The Challenge of
Outward Bound

By the same author

Youth Looks at the World
Education and Colonial Policy
The Next Step in Canadian Education
Education and Crisis
A Philosophy for the Teacher
Universities in the Modern World

The Challenge of Outward Bound

BASIL FLETCHER

Professor Emeritus, The University of Leeds
Research Fellow, The University of Bristol

HEINEMANN : LONDON

William Heinemann Ltd
15 Queen St, Mayfair, London WIX 8BE
LONDON MELBOURNE TORONTO
JOHANNESBURG AUCKLAND

© Outward Bound Trust 1971
First published 1971
434 90566 6

Printed in Great Britain by Morrison and Gibb Ltd.
London and Edinburgh

FOREWORD

by Sir Spencer Summers
Chairman, Outward Bound Management Committee

The idea of trying to assess the effect of Outward Bound training by an independent trained mind was one of the principal outcomes of the two-day Conference held at Harrogate in May 1965. At that same Conference, Sir Alec Clegg, Director of Education for the West Riding, paid a generous tribute to Outward Bound by saying that, through this application of Kurt Hahn's philosophy, education had been given a new dimension.

This book will help to explain what he meant.

It is reasonable to suppose that the conviction with which St. Paul conveyed the Christian message was enhanced by the fact that he started as an aggressive disbeliever. Although Professor Fletcher started as a mere sceptic, this description of how and why he became a real enthusiast may well also carry weight on that account.

Over the years, there have been two dominant propositions potentially adverse to Outward Bound claims which have been voiced from time to time. The first asserts that four weeks must be too short a time in which to produce anything more than a transitory impact. The research here recorded into the persistence of the effect

v

of the training provides a complete answer to this type of disbeliever.

The second asserts that an artificially provided challenge in natural surroundings must be so far removed from the normal life of those coming from factories, offices or the public services that the experience can have little relevance to the social and other problems with which they will surely be confronted. One of the most interesting and encouraging conclusions reached by Professor Fletcher is that the experience of an Outward Bound Course is even more relevant to everyday life now than when it was first introduced thirty years ago.

One other point warrants special mention—the Staff. The tribute paid to the dedication, teaching ability, and imagination of the Staff at the Schools is as welcome as it is deserved. Outward Bound is essentially about people. Unless the Staff contrive to bring about a real rapport with those in their care they will fail to kindle that spark of enthusiasm, perhaps even idealism, so essential to success. The extent to which this assessment of Outward Bound may be called success is the measure of the credit due to the Staff, whose personal relationship with those who come on Outward Bound Courses is everything.

I should like to take this opportunity of thanking publicly the Joseph Rowntree Memorial Trust, through whose financial help the research work carried out by Professor Fletcher was made possible. To him we are particularly indebted for all the time and trouble he took, and not least for the wisdom and the charm with which he describes the fulfilment of his assignment.

PREFACE

This broad survey of the work of six schools could not have been brought to completion without the generous help of many individuals, most of whom were already giving freely of their limited spare time to the work of the Outward Bound Trust. The list of those who contributed their time, energy, and encouragement is given elsewhere in this volume, under the heading of Acknowledgments. I should have liked, except for consideration of space, to have placed all their names on a record but the list is very large, especially of those hundreds of past students of the Outward Bound Schools who wrote short or often very long letters to me. I thank them all with great sincerity and wish their work for the Schools every success in the future. I am reminded by this of the bold and humorous words spoken by Winston Churchill in August 1940, looking into the future of a different but not unrelated enterprise. He said this:

'For my own part, looking out upon the future, I do not view the process with any misgivings. I could not stop it if I wished; no one can stop it. Like the Mississippi it will keep rolling along. Let it roll, in full flood, inexorable, irresistible, benignant, to broader lands and better days.'

One of the reasons why it occurred to me to call this

volume the 'Challenge' of Outward Bound was because, among the memories of Latin that remain like a faint dust on the surface of my mind is one that reminds me that the word 'challenge' comes from the Latin *calumnia*, a word which, to say the least, has a critical ring about it. And I began to study the work of the Outward Bound Schools in a distinctly critical frame of mind, because, in addition to my own deep ignorance of their work, I had heard them either praised or denigrated in, it seemed to me, extravagant or emotional terms. So that when a friend, neighbour, and member of the Council of my University, Sir Wilfred Anson, invited me to make such a study it was the last thing that I wanted to do. Only my admiration for him and my respect for his office persuaded me to accept his invitation. Nevertheless, I have never, since that day, or for a moment, regretted that decision, for it has had the effect of adding wonderfully and richly to my circle of friends. Some of these I list by name under Acknowledgments but I have not included in that list the names of the six Wardens of the British Schools and my brief tributes to them in the text of the book are quite inadequate. In moments when my mind is unusually 'fancy-free' I invent an Outward Bound Course of a more extravagant kind than any that has yet been born of the very inventive minds of the Wardens themselves. It is one held during a Parliamentary recess and designed for the total membership of the British Cabinet; but—and this is the important point of the Course—it is staffed by the six Wardens of the Schools acting under the direction of a distinguished ex-Warden. A little firmer than this fanciful Course is my belief that it might, in fact, sharpen the cutting-edge of political leadership in Great Britain.

There are two other names that I might have included in my list of Acknowledgments—but I should like to refer to these at slightly greater length, partly because

both have contributed greatly to the philosophy of the
Outward Bound Movement and partly because my meetings with them were under circumstances that, for me,
were dramatic. It was Charles Haddon Chambers who
coined the phrase 'the long arm of coincidence' and I
have never known it longer than in relation to my meetings with these two men. Although the Outward Bound
Movement is very British in its healthy practicality, both
of these men were foreigners and both more visionary
than the typical Briton. One name is that of the oldest
and the other of almost the youngest who have given
unstintingly of their time and thought to the work of the
Schools: the first name is that of the German, Kurt Hahn,
and the second of the African, John Lubega.

When I began to study the work of the Schools in 1967
I thought I had never met anyone seriously involved in
their work. This was not the case for I had met both
Kurt Hahn and John Lubega at twenty-year intervals in
a way that demonstrates how long indeed is the arm of
coincidence.

In 1932 Kurt Hahn, then Headmaster of Schule
Schloss Salem, invited me to bring over an English
hockey team to play the eleven of his school, which, in
that year, had had an unbroken record of success. We
played at Salem and afterwards (having given them their
first defeat) went on a short tour of western Germany. By
a series of strange mistakes we found ourselves alone in a
long express train that had actually been prepared to carry
Hitler and his martial entourage. The police, learning of
a Communist plot to blow up the train, had sent Hitler
and his gang by road but alas, to expose the plot, sent on
the (as they supposed) empty train over the mined route.
Happily the timing of the bombs was faulty and we
reached England safely, as did also, in the year following,
Kurt Hahn himself. That vivid incident was linked in my
mind with a note I made of something Hahn said then

about his school and which he might have applied, eight years later, to the first Outward Bound School which he and Lawrence Holt of the Blue Funnel Line founded in Wales. He said then: 'In this School there is no room for the discords which are the curse of Germany. Our aim is to lay the foundations of class peace and of religious peace. We want to educate citizens not subjects, qualified for international co-operation.'

In 1950, when I was teaching at a school at Masaka on the shores of Lake Victoria in Uganda (and unknown to me a small African boy, John Lubega, was also at his primary school at Masaka), I began to introduce into my physical education periods 'adventure training' of the kind then being pioneered in Africa by W. H. White, who later wrote his standard work on *Physical Education in Tropical Africa*. I was quite unconscious that John Lubega was inspired at this time to aim at a career in physical education, but so it was. His way forward was very hard for a poor boy from a village school but by intelligence, force of character, and personal athletic ability he struggled forward and finally found a place as a teacher of physical education at Nairobi in Kenya, where White's work made Lubega's expertise both appreciated and wanted. When the East African Outward Bound School was set up at Loitokitok, John became its first Senior Instructor. His contribution to the philosophy of the Outward Bound Movement came when, jointly with Geoffrey Salisbury of the Royal Commonwealth Society for the Blind, he planned a bold initiative that would give practical form to the new but growing aim of the movement to assist the physically handicapped. They planned an ascent of Kilimanjaro, the African mountain which is higher than Mont Blanc, by a party of blind African climbers. John Lubega led two blind students from Tanzania, two from Kenya, and three from Uganda up the weary slog to the beginnings of the snow and ice and then with great care to the very top itself. As they rested on the summit and, in their joy, cried out 'Now we must ask Sir John Hunt to take us to the top of Everest', a passing East African Airways plane dipped its wings in salute. So too, I should like also to salute all those, from Kurt Hahn to John Lubega, who have worked and struggled to bring to maturity a group of schools that now number no less than twenty-seven and that grow in influence with every passing year.

ACKNOWLEDGMENTS

1. The research described in Chapters 5 and 9 of the text was made possible by a grant from the Joseph Rowntree Memorial Trust. The Secretary of the Trust, Lewis Waddilove, gave much personal encouragement particularly at difficult points in the progress of the research.

2. Valuable criticism and guidance came from an Outward Bound Research Advisory Committee set up by the University of Bristol School of Education and particularly from Professor William Taylor, Dr. John Taylor, and Mr. John Lang, of the School.

3. The officers of the Outward Bound Trust made freely available to the author their records and files. They hid nothing. They even sent records which showed where, at times (and as in the best-regulated families), experiments had gone off at 'half-cock' or advances were retarded by personal disagreements. In particular, unstinted help was given by Sir Spencer Summers, Commander Hugh Jenkinson, and Johnnie Johnson.

4. Chapter 8 on City Challenge owes a very great deal to the collaboration of Jim Hogan, Deputy Education Officer for the West Riding of Yorkshire, and John

Taylor, Director of Education for the City of Leeds. Both were deeply involved in and responsible for the success of the first City Challenge Course held in the City of Leeds.

5. Martin Hardcastle, who, following his retirement from work as Housemaster and Deputy Headmaster of Clifton College, undertook an 'internal' survey of the work of the six British Outward Bound Schools on behalf of the Trust, most generously allowed much material used in Chapter 2 to be abstracted from his Research Report. In addition, the grant from the Rowntree Trust made it possible for visits to be undertaken to the Schools in his company, when he was able to provide invaluable information about the history of the Schools and the story of their overseas developments.

ILLUSTRATIONS

GENERAL

CITY CHALLENGE

SCHOOLS IN U.K.

CONTENTS

1. ORIGINS

I had written and published seven books before I began to work on the present volume, the eighth, which came to be written in a totally different way from the other seven. It can almost be said to have had a life of its own, and to insist on being written, when I was half-way through preparing a detailed statistical research report for the University of Bristol. In that research report my aim was to be objective, logical, and statistical, but, as its writing proceeded, all sorts of subjective and imaginative ideas kept on rising into consciousness and I was only able to get on with my statistical study by jotting down the intrusive ideas on separate sheets of paper. It is these jottings that have been woven into the fabric of this book.

My statistical study was made during 1968 and 1969 and the research report was published in 1970. Before I began to write it I had read with great profit a publication of the Outward Bound Trust produced in 1969 called *A Report on Outward Bound*, by Martin Hardcastle, which was designed to review the practice of each Outward Bound School in turn and to recommend any changes that might seem to be required in our rapidly changing educational scene. My own report was designed to be more detached than that of Martin Hardcastle, for, unlike him, I started in complete ignorance of the work of the schools. He knew them well but I had never visited any nor met any of their wardens or a single member of their numerous staff. If anything, I started with a prejudice against them because I had half-listened to a rumble of criticism by condescending dons in university senior common rooms which, as I later discovered, was generally based on an ignorance as complete as my own.

In my own report, I deliberately excluded all personal views and attitudes, merely summarizing the views and judgements of some 3,000 students (and the organizations who sponsored them) who, with 20,000 others, had passed through the schools over a five-year period. I wanted the percentages, the averages, and the trends of the research report to speak for themselves, with no particular supporting argument from me. I believe they did this, but like all statistical analyses they presented only one facet of the truth, many aspects of which are lost when it is strained through a numerical mesh. Representative figures have to be derived from 'statistical populations' of from 2,000 to 3,000 and in the process individual differences are necessarily levelled out. Yet 90 per cent of the truth about human beings relates to their separate and distinct individual characteristics. In addition to these two distortions, statistics ignore that blend of value, attitude, imagination, and sensibility that makes all discussion of educational issues both human and humane. The result of all this was that what I had expressed technically, I found I had also to try to say in human terms.

As I collected my statistics about the work and influence of Outward Bound Schools two discoveries deepened my conviction that I must make an evaluative as well as an objective study. My first discovery was that in the years following 1960, after nearly twenty years of steady growth, the Outward Bound movement began to show all the signs of an educational rebirth. During those twenty years the original and creative thinking that had given birth first to the Sea School at Aberdovey and then to five more schools in Scotland, England and Wales, had changed and developed as, in one school after another, the original concepts and techniques were revised and enlarged by creative-minded school wardens, able, and given freedom to adapt and invent. But during this time nothing radically new or different was attempted. Orthodox methods were retained because they had been tried and found successful. But from 1960 onwards the picture changes, new types of course appear, old types are radically modified, new experiments and new ideas of many kinds begin to produce a ferment in a work which for many years had been accepted without much critical review. The young men in the movement particularly, new wardens and new instructors (as well as some old men) were everywhere open to new ideas, eager to try them out, and, more important still, were, when I began my survey, being given the freedom and the means to do so.

My second discovery, and it was also unexpected, was the realization that what had begun as a simple wartime educational expedient in 1941 had, after twenty-nine years, and in a totally different world, become astonishingly relevant to that world.

When the first Outward Bound School was opened in 1941 at Aberdovey in north-west Wales, the simple aim was to provide a rigorous, adventurous, pre-sea training course for young men who might go on to help to win the Battle of the Atlantic. The first students in 1941 needed no lectures to persuade them of the importance of the objectives of their education. Overwhelmingly, they were anxious to do what lay in their power to help their fellow-citizens who were hard pressed in war and facing the real possibilities of starvation and invasion.

When the war ended in 1945, and for some years afterwards, the task of the warden and staff of Aberdovey Sea School was straightforward and its educational objectives clear. The civilized world had been brought to the brink of barbarism by a rich and educated nation that had allowed itself to be dominated by a perverse and evil man. To avoid a recurrence of this disaster, the rising generation must be armed against the infection of totalitarianism. All of those concerned with education—parents, teachers, youth workers, educational administrators and employers—must devote themselves to the production of critical minds, avoiding dogma and never lending themselves to the indoctrination of the young.

Together with much that was admirable in this post-war educational vision, it can now with hindsight be seen that there was much simplicity, even naivety, in the belief that freed from authoritarian impositions the young men and women of the 1940s and 1950s would strive after the best that lay within their grasp. What the teachers of these two decades did not realize, and perhaps could not have realized, was that the education of the post-war generation would have to take place amid a widespread abandonment of nearly all the moral and religious beliefs that had been accepted during their own youth.

The world of 1970 is very different from the world of 1950. After the Second World War there was a revulsion not only against authoritarianism in government but also against all forms of authority, whether expressed by parents, teachers or what came soon to be called 'the establishment'.

In the twenty-six years since the end of the Second World War there has been an unparalleled growth in technology and its related skills. But there has been no direct connection between this vast increase of 'means' and the 'ends' they exist to serve, which may be defined very briefly as 'the good society'. If individuals are to be formed to serve the good society and to maintain its quality they will have to possess a certain unity of self, and certain ways of thinking and feeling, more or less coherent, rich, and sensitive. It is in the sources of this that there has been, in the modern world, such contraction. What lasts from an educational experience is not the enhancement of memory but the enhancement of being. But it is beliefs about the nature of man, what he may become and what is his destiny, with the morality that flows from these, that enhance a man's being. Of course, such beliefs must be adequate to the nature and complexity of the modern world. They must combine sanity with sincerity and be held with some degree of passion. Alas, the modern mind does not possess these old certainties! It is distrustful of self and so has come to distrust nearly all the beliefs that are essential for the maintenance of civilized thought and conduct.

This modern sceptical mood has descended in a particular way upon the British people. The lassitude following two world wars; the disillusionment at finding the nation worse off on the winning than on the losing side; the contraction of horizons following the loss of an empire and the failure as yet to find a new national purpose in serving a united Europe; the blatant materialism and cupidity of the instruments of mass communication; all these influences and more are bearing hardly upon a nation for so long accustomed to act pragmatically and to think creatively in the pursuit of a known and admired national purpose.

This loss of purpose has blunted the attack on five aspects of national well-being and unless this attack is resumed, social weakness and loss of purpose may be destructive, perhaps totally destructive, of national life. These five problems can be put briefly as follows:

    1. the great increase in crimes of violence by the young and the readiness of pressure groups to use violence

and even murder or threats of murder to achieve
their ends;

2. the accelerating destruction of the natural environment;

3. the softness of character and boredom of mood that results from the combination of unprecedented security and affluence with unparalleled freedom from restraint;

4. the growth of a substantial minority of adolescents who do not accept the responsibilities of adult life but still feel free to live on the labour of others;

5. the increase of industrial disorder and strikes, due to the increasing abdication of vigorous leadership by both organized management and trade unions, separately and jointly.

As I came to know more of the work of the Outward Bound Schools I saw increasingly that both the tactics and strategy of their work were related to the solution of these five pressing social problems. This only became clear to me as the piece of survey work which I had begun as an almost routine scientific survey drew to its close.

The nature of this survey can best be described by quoting from a memorandum which was prepared by the Outward Bound Trust in 1967 in an appeal for a research grant. This stated:

'By 1967 it was felt that the time had come to take stock of what the Trust was doing and of the effect on those who attend its courses. A large pool of experience exists upon which to draw from differing sites and differing interpretations of the Outward Bound concept by differing personalities. It is also recognized that times have changed significantly during the development period, entailing a corresponding need to consider whether the work of the Trust needs further adaptation.

'Another motive behind the idea of a stocktaking exercise was the knowledge that the Trust is in process of embarking on entirely new ways of presenting established principles and is considering quite dramatic experiments to widen the sphere within which Outward Bound operates. Two examples may be given to illustrate this point—

'In July 1967 a Course known as CITY CHALLENGE was arranged in Leeds, in co-operation with the Leeds City Council, the staff being drawn from Outward Bound and the Local Authority. Whilst there was an element of the traditional outdoor activities such as rock climbing and canoeing, the main opportunity for challenge took the form of participating in a series of social service activities. These included helping in the Casualty Ward at the hospital and in the Salvation Army hostel for "down and outs"; assisting with immigrant children during the morning break; cleaning out insanitary, occupied dwellings, some of whose occupants had refused access to the Welfare authorities; building an "adventure" playground in a new housing estate; redecorating old people's houses, and training for Civil Defence. The impact is quite outstanding, and further demonstrations of the possibilities of Outward Bound in an urban context have been planned.

'Then there are certain times of the year when for various reasons it is difficult to fill all the schools completely. At these times it has been decided to encourage the schools to run new types of courses as experiments, either in parallel with their reduced normal courses, or by transferring their normal intake to the other schools. Amongst the different courses already undertaken are short courses for students at colleges of education, for young people on probation with their probation officers and approved school boys with their masters, also special courses for particular athletic teams aimed at a mental as well as physical toning up. Another type of course is the extension course in which a group of ex-students are invited to pursue more deeply both the activities and

attitudes to which they were introduced on their ordinary
Outward Bound course.

'Thought is being given to the possibilities of special
courses for handicapped young people to which would be
invited ex-Outward Bound students who might be
attracted to the idea of giving the additional help that
would obviously be needed. Other possibilities include
the running of special types of courses in collaboration
with local Education Authorities.'

2. THE SCHOOLS IN GREAT BRITAIN

There are six and only six Outward Bound Schools in Great Britain and they are not schools in the ordinary sense since they run many different types of courses for groups of young men and women with different needs. The standard course, their *raison d'être*, is a course of twenty-six days, run for a group of about 100 between the ages of sixteen and nineteen years. Since it is so central to the work of the Schools the standard course will be described in sufficient detail for later research work to be understood; but before doing this, a word or two needs to be written about each of the six schools, since the first thing that strikes the visitor is the very great similarity of aim and principle between them all and the second is how very different each is from the other.

I found work in the Schools well organized and discipline firm, yet the whole spirit and atmosphere at each school proclaimed that there was freedom—from rules, from hierarchy, from class and racial distinctions (there were one or two black faces on every course). The feeling of freedom is difficult to describe but it seems to be in the very air you breathe.

The first school I visited, and the first school to be founded, was the Outward Bound Sea School at Aberdovey on the west coast of Wales. If you start from Bristol you travel across the superb empty mountain

9

country of Radnorshire, then down the leafy Dovey valley until the sand beaches and blue sea and noise of the surf off the estuary bar warn you that you are approaching the little fishing port of Aberdovey. The sight of a line of brightly coloured canoes drawn up in the reeds and a rocking dinghy or two on the water warn you that an Outward Bound School is at hand—up a steep road between terraced gardens, almost hidden by tall trees.

The full picture of life at Aberdovey in its early years has been recorded by its first Warden, Jim Hogan, now Deputy Education Officer in the West Riding; it was published by Educational Productions Limited in 1968 under the title *Impelled into Experiences*. Hogan was helped in those early and difficult years between 1941 and 1945 by a Dr. Zimmerman, a refugee from Nazi tyranny who had been the Director of Physical Education at Gottingen University. Zimmerman was far more interested in the diffident and clumsy boy than in the gifted athlete and this early note struck at Aberdovey has been a continuing thread in the life of all the schools since. It is a point worth mentioning right at the outset, because in my talks with hundreds of individuals in the course of my research survey I kept on hearing the criticisms that the schools glorified physical achievement, that they were only for the tough, or that they aimed at producing a muscle-bound élite. I discovered that this was far from the truth. Zimmerman's early emphasis on the need for the quite ordinary student to discover his hidden reserves of energy and for the physically inept to overcome their weaknesses has a modern echo in the following terse phrase taken from a current issue of the prospectus of the Moray Sea School in Scotland: 'The Warden will accept the physically handicapped including those suffering from polio, the deaf and dumb, and the blind'.

Another important feature of the life of all the Schools began quite early at Aberdovey. This was the system of teaching by small groups. Because Aberdovey was a Sea School, the groups were called watches and each watch consisted of from ten to twelve students. This decentralized system of teaching was also linked with the system of self-government. In each watch, a captain, a vice-captain, a steward responsible for kit, and a first-aid officer responsible for safety precautions were appointed, in the first instance for a week, by the warden. At the end of the week new 'officers' were elected freely by secret ballot from the members of the watch. So watch discipline (in the broad sense of organization and order) became the concern jointly of the watch instructor working closely with his captain and vice-captain. Then, for each course, a court consisting of all the captains and vice-captains met to discuss 'course' organization and discipline with the warden and his instructors, as occasion needed, and generally oversaw its progress.

At Aberdovey I had enjoyed the hospitality of Captain Fuller—known always as 'Freddie' at the school and to his friends. Captain Fuller is the most senior of all the wardens and when I talked to him he was looking forward to a busy retirement after almost thirty years of work at the Sea School. Fuller went to sea at fifteen years of age and had a hard time during the economic depression of the 1930s when, with his master's ticket, he failed, like so many more good navigators, to get a ship. His luck turned when he joined the Holt line of ships and met Lawrence Holt, for both talked with growing enthusiasm of the need for a sea-training that would prepare young men not only for life at sea but for many other walks of life. In this basic idea they foreshadowed one of the fundamental principles of Outward Bound training—to use sailing or climbing or canoeing to train, not for a life of work or leisure spent at sea or on mountain and river, but for life itself.

After a few hours spent with Captain Fuller I knew I

had met a simple and selfless character, quite unself-conscious but with a deep concern for those whose lives had run into a patch of rough water or had to be spent in cramped and narrowing shadows. As early as 1956 he had written something, as I know from my own work in Leeds, that had led him on to design the first City Challenge Course, which would replace the challenge of the sea by the challenge of urban decay. In 1956 he wrote: 'What of our Borstals, Approved Schools and Prisons. Do not they contain some who would be more quickly salvaged by such a course as Outward Bound?' Ten years later this line of thought led his mind away from the beauty of the west coast of Wales to the ugliness of the slums of Leeds and to the planning of a new type of Outward Bound Course. With dogged persistence, and in the face of doubt, criticism, and some outright op-position, he finally got his imaginative plans for a City Course afloat and steered the first one through some difficult waters. Now, after four years and many courses, the City Challenge Courses have proved their worth—for some who would regard sea-training as offensively hearty, for others whose personal needs are better met in cities than in the lonely countryside, and, not least, for those who wait for death in a geriatric ward or beat against the prison walls of their minds in a mental hospital.

As I drove away from Aberdovey I reflected on my first meeting with an Outward Bound warden. I suppose I had built up a fanciful image of what such a man might be like—a sort of cross between the games captain of a public school and an army physical-training instructor. But at Aberdovey I had met a man whose early games had not been played on the sunlit lawns of a public school but on the dirty lower deck of a tramp steamer; and as I went on to meet one after another of the six wardens I realized that my fanciful 'warden-image' could hardly have been wider of the truth. It is true that all struck me as being supremely fit physically and all clearly loved the countryside and life in the open air, but this seemed to be about all they had in common. It was their differences that struck me rather than any similarities, and each was of such strength of personality as to be quite impossible to fit into any 'type' or 'image'. I certainly never thought that I should be meeting, as I went on from school to school (to select a single, no doubt untypical, characteristic of each warden in turn) an urban social reformer, a teacher of dancing, a painter from the Royal Academy School, an Oxford philosopher, an air-force officer with an agricultural training, and a professional soldier with experience as a teacher in a school for maladjusted children. Later, I saw that the six wardens had many more qualities of experience and outlook than those I mention, but I never met the Outward Bound Warden 'type'.

The second Outward Bound School to be founded was Eskdale in the Lake District. The Outward Bound Trust had been set up in 1946 and in 1949 a loan made it possible to buy a large country property where the kind of education developed at Aberdovey might be adapted to life in the mountains, with the skill of mountaineering replacing the skill of seamanship. Lord Rea's old home, 'Gatehouse', set in a splendid garden on a small lake, was bought for what today sounds the ridiculous price of £15,000. After adaptation, the Eskdale Mountain School was opened in 1950 by the Minister of Education. I, myself, came to Eskdale School after a drive up the hairpin bends of a minor road and a brief climb up the Langdale Pikes, which give, I think, the best mountain views in England; so I saw at once how wise had been the choice of location for the second Outward Bound School.

It was at the Eskdale School in 1951 that the first Outward Bound course for girls was held—the first of the many courses that were to lead, in time, to the opening of a Girls' Outward Bound School at Towyn in Wales. It was at Eskdale, too, as soon as a 'mountaineering' programme had settled down, that a more general statement of the objectives of Outward Bound training was defined. This statement, later developed and modified as one new school after another adapted and modified the original Aberdovey programme, was expressed in the words:

'The Schools must be founded on the following principles. They must be residential and courses must last for a minimum of four weeks. They must be open to all, based on a spiritual foundation, and must contain a diversity of occupations and nationalities, without political or sectarian bias. They must present each student with a set of conditions, and give him, possibly for the first time, the opportunity to discover himself. These conditions, self-discipline, team-work, adventure, physical hardship and some risk, are rarely met with except in time of war. They must endeavour to develop character through training with a vocational or other practical interest.'

By the time that I came to visit the Eskdale Mountain School I had ceased to expect that the warden would be a hearty extrovert, and certainly Roger Putnam at Eskdale was the least like this false image. As I talked to him it was difficult to believe that we were not colleagues in a university senior common room. This was because there was an academic serenity, a simplicity, and a critical-mindedness about him which seemed to flow over into his staff and students. If his philosophical training at Oxford has made Roger Putnam critical of all shallow educational enthusiasm I soon realized that this also made him a very forward-looking warden. He followed his Modern Greats at Oxford with a period as a planning officer for the Middlesex County Council and this has also directed his mind towards the future and to the attempt to achieve a balance of tidy administration with radical new development.

In 1952 a third school was opened on the north coast of Scotland. When I came to the Moray Sea School at Burghead on a dull rainy November day I found the little fishing port of dark grey houses, the tossing fishing vessels in the harbour, and the bleak church, all rather dour and forbidding. A stiff wind blew across the rocky granite headlands so that even the coast looked grim—but later, when the sun shone, I found it first tolerable and then attractive. I realized then, as I remembered the lovely Highland mountains over which I had come, that Burghead was a well chosen site, right on the cliff tops but with unending miles of magnificent hill and mountain behind to be explored and climbed.

When the Ministry of Defence decided to set up its Norway Outward Bound Training Centre for N.A.T.O. forces in Europe they appointed to be the head of what would obviously become a centre for sea, mountain and snow training, a young officer who had trained the first Army Pentathlon Team to win a gold medal in Europe. From this pioneer work in Norway, Gordon Richards, now Warden of the Moray Sea School, was persuaded to undertake another piece of experimental education under the rather freer condition of an Outward Bound School and this was the application of his own original ideas in physical education to the basic preparatory work of a standard course. From this work at Moray, Gordon Richards has now gone on to a different field of experiment—that of the welfare courses described in a later chapter. An enthusiasm for physical education was not the only enthusiasm that Gordon Richards brought from his pre-army experiences. He had indeed been a master in charge of physical education at a boy's boarding school but he had also, for a time, been a teacher at a school for maladjusted children.

I remembered this fact on my first visit when I saw the individual care and sympathy he was giving to a drug addict and a juvenile delinquent who were students on a standard course. Later I learnt much more about his welfare courses for juvenile delinquents and these are briefly described in Chapter 7. At my first visit I picked up a great many new ideas, but decided that, in my slower English way, I must examine these away from his Celtic enthusiasm—and I came away considerably stimulated.

In 1955 grants from various trusts made it possible for the Outward Bound Trust to consider establishing a second mountain school to match the two sea schools. A dignified eighteenth-century house that had become an hotel was discovered about half-way along the western shore of Lake Ullswater between Patterdale and Penrith. I came to the Ullswater Mountain School through the mists of the mountain pass of Kirkstone, whence you drop steeply down to the picturesque little village of Patterdale and to the lakeside road which in my view is the finest road in the Lake District, and perhaps in England. Through the trees you get bright glimpses of the long winding oval of Lake Ullswater with its hills dropping very steeply to the water's edge.

It was here that I came across the first striking evidence of the quality of students who had taken courses in the period 1964 to 1969. This evidence is best given in the form of an extract from a letter, written by the victim of a car accident on the road along which I drove, whose plight was discovered by a group returning to the school after a climb in the hills. He wrote:

'We had a very bad car smash on the Ullswater road but fortunately a group of boys returning from a climb arrived at the scene of the smash. The boys used a fire-extinguisher to prevent petrol from igniting. They phoned for doctor, ambulance and police in that order, provided us with warm coverings, first aid treatment and rapidly boiled water to make hot drinks. The boys, when they left, gave neither names nor addresses but quietly went on their way as we were taken to hospital. Their kindness, consideration and efficiency is something that we shall long remember and speaks very highly of the training and instruction they receive at the School.'

It was at Ullswater, too, that I talked to some of those who had not long returned from the first course for students from a British School to be mounted in a European country. 'Operation Luxembourg', as this was called, is described in Chapter 7.

It was service in the Royal Air Force that led the Warden of Ullswater Mountain School to abandon his career as an agricultural scientist and to embark on adventure training. One of the first things you see at Ullswater when you leave the friendly staff common room is the wind-sock on its helicopter landing strip, and prob-ably the second is the unusually well designed projects room, with much evidence on display of the work of students in the exploration of their environment. Both are indications of the way in which Lester Davies, the Warden of Ullswater, has developed two aspects of the standard course as only a man with the combination of R.A.F. and agricultural training could—air-mountain rescue skills with specially designed equipment, and environmental studies by a project method. I met students at Ullswater, from the narrow streets of industrial cities, who were having their eyes opened both to the poten-tialities of the air and to the destruction of the countryside, for the first time in their lives.

By 1959 two gaps in the provision of Outward Bound Schools began to be appreciated. There was no school in the southern half of England; and it was not satisfactory for all courses for girls to be held at Eskdale or at one of three or four other temporary centres. Finance for a school wholly for girls was not at this time assured, because although senior management in industry had come to realize that the cost of courses for boys seconded from industry was a sound investment, it did not hold a similar view for girls. However, the members of the Trust in London were in the mood to take some degree of risk when they found a large house, Holne Park, surrounded by 60 acres of parkland in one of the finest scenic positions in a county, the county of Devon, well endowed with such delights. It was not very far from the south coast of Devon and behind it stretched the heather-covered hills of Dartmoor. Along its boundary ran the River Dart, one of the finest canoeing rivers in England. Unlike the day of my arrival at the Moray School, my visit to Holne Park, the first of many, fell on a bright midsummer day, so that I was forced to stop and enjoy the reflected sunlight dancing on the rapids and whirlpools of the Dart just by the gates of the school. As I paused at a high narrow bridge, a line of runners from the school, on their way back from an expedition, paused at the top of the bridge and one by one clambered over the parapet and dropped the long 30 feet into the dark waters of the deep pool below. One runner, dripping wet, returned to the bridge to give some gentle encouragement to a few hesitant boys at the parapet. I asked him if he really liked this kind of frightening exercise. 'Yes', he replied. 'Now that I've done that, I know I can do anything.'

However, it was not so much the adventurous aspect of the work at the Devon Outward Bound School that made a deep impression on me as the immense patience that was shown by one instructor with one or two non-swimmers at the outdoor heated swimming pool. A patrol were having a period of practice in 'drownproofing' or learning to stay afloat upright in deep water with no movement except that of the head as this is raised rhythmically to take in breath. One of the non-swimmers had a pathological fear of water and needed some help even to get in at the shallow end holding on to the side of the bath. By the end of the hour he was at the deep end, even if still holding on to the side, and before I left the school he had learnt to swim. As I watched this single boy I realized that the work begun by Zimmerman at Aberdovey was still bearing fruit in Devon twenty-five years later.

It was on my first visit to Holne Park that I began to look more closely at the work of the schools for the 3 or 4 per cent of their students who are sent by the Home Office from Approved Schools or Borstals. There is never more than one in a team of ten or twelve boys, his sponsorship is kept a close secret, and he is asked not to disclose it himself. In this way he can often shake off for a time the burden of his past and live a normal life with normal boys of his own age. I was allowed to know who were the juvenile delinquents on one Devon course and I found that by its end all, without exception, were speaking strongly of their appreciation of the experience. One of these boys, the most intelligent, wrote afterwards to the warden of the school, and because he was better able than most to describe and analyse his experience his letter is worth quoting in full. Ideally, all juvenile delinquents should be given the chance to recover, in a situation of small group education, as a minority among non-delinquents, and it would seem to be the worst of all possible treatments to shut them up with scores of other young criminals in an unadventurous environment. This letter from one young delinquent incidentally gives a good picture of life at the school, seen through the eyes of a single student.

'From the moment of arrival at the Outward Bound School I had a feeling that I would be inferior compared with other lads there. Colleges and Public Schools and trainee seamen, soldiers, airmen and policemen in my idea were more intelligent and sophisticated than I was and I thought that I would be left out of things as far as company was concerned. No one knew in fact that I was from Borstal, but there was just this feeling I had of not being up to their standards.

'However as soon as I was settled in and got to know a few christian names I found that my earlier conclusion of the place and people was totally unjust. Everyone was so helpful towards one another and so friendly. I think what really helped out a lot was the fact that my physical capabilities were higher than those of other lads. This showed when for the first five evenings we did an outdoor circuit training session called "Runabout" and the other lads of my patrol seemingly looked up to me as if I were setting an example and they all were dying to reach the amount of repetitions and speed at which I did things.

'This was a tremendous boost of confidence for me. Now I felt secure with the lads there and that I would be accepted in many groups of people from any walk of life. It's a marvellous feeling or part of life to be liked by other people and respected for what you are. These lads I really had respect for and a great sense of comrade-ship. I know they were more intelligent in fact through Degrees and well recognised examinations that they had passed, yet my respect for them was exactly the same as their's for me. I think I gained a terrific amount of social qualities from them that I didn't have before. I am not very well travelled and can say that the only close friends I had before I came here were the ones I had grown up with.

'There is so much to be gained from mixing with and meeting people from different backgrounds. It broadens one's outlook on life and gives a great deal of knowledge about the human race. Before I would have shunned high class and Public School; this I know now was only through ignorance.

'The course itself was very exciting, many of the activities I had never taken part in and never dreamt I would ever do some of them, climbing, hiking over tens of miles, potholing and surf canoeing. The canoeing and climbing I intend very much to carry on with in one way or another through youth movements, etc. The challenge of climbing a two hundred foot sheer cliff is quite something to someone who has never even worn a pair of climbing boots or tied a bowline before. I wouldn't say it is exactly thrilling or frightening, just a great challenge and its got to be met. The amount of self satisfaction one gets from this sort of things is tremendous. For me, five minutes before, the cliff I had climbed seemed totally impossible, yet I had done it. I didn't know my own capability; yet now I felt confident, not reckless at all, but very careful and was sure I knew where to stop when my limit was reached.

'The hiking I would have thought was just a matter of walking and keeping going. Yet again, the companionship part comes into it, where you can comfort one another and give encouragement and take criticism. The "Final Scheme" I did was a seventy mile hike across Exmoor and Dartmoor with three other lads. Everything was rosy for the first few miles and then blisters appeared by the dozen and tiredness spelt misery with lack of will-power to go on. I think I would never attempt the hike on my own, the boredom and frustration would be too great to stand. With a team spirit and a good bunch of lads anything is possible. No one's true colours are shown I don't think, until hardship and suffering creep in. If I had a job to walk it was wonderful to have beside me someone I knew I could lean on and vice versa.

'Altogether I think I have benefited a great deal from the course. Personal satisfaction of being awarded a badge, something well worth while working for. Knowing my physical capabilities to a much greater extent than before and my much broader mind having dealt with these many fine people. A fine course and fully recommended to anyone who wants to learn something about himself.'

At Holne Park I met the new Warden of the Devon School, Derek Pritchard, who had just arrived from East Africa, where he had been Warden of the Mountain School at Loitokitok. He had not yet moved into the Warden's House and was living in a caravan which had a 'safari' look about it. Just as it was the possession of contrasting qualities that had struck me about the first two wardens I had met, so, at my third meeting, it was the feeling that the new warden at Holne Park brought the contrast of both imaginative and practical qualities of mind to a new work. Derek Pritchard was trained to be a painter at the Royal Academy School of Painting in London and apart from the fact that the impact of the Second World War broke up his career, he would almost certainly have become a painter or a teacher of painting. His experience in the Parachute Regiment turned his mind in the direction of adventure training and he became experienced in this sort of training, first as the instructor at the Eskdale Mountain School and then as the executive officer at the Citizenship and Leadership Training College in Nigeria. He is the first warden to bring back to the British scene a view of Outward Bound educational principles formed by experience in West and East Africa. He is also the first example of an Outward Bound warden who has been recruited from inside the movement. This is an important precedent. Any organization or movement can easily become inbred and this often happens, but it must offer a career structure to its teachers and a majority of these must feel that there is a way forward to the highest posts if they are not to grow discouraged.

For four years, separate courses for boys and for girls were held at the Devon School, but by 1963 the feminists in the Outward Bound Trust pressed successfully for the foundation of a school wholly for girls. A suitable large house was found in Wales, conveniently placed a few miles northward along the coast from the Aberdovey Sea School. Like Aberdovey, it was a family house of some character, perched up a steep hill, with a view of the sea, in a setting of gardens and trees. Its proximity to Aberdovey clearly made contacts and collaboration possible.

Before my first visit to Rhowniar I had had doubts about the applicability of courses of the Outward Bound type to girls, although I knew that in modifying the standard course programme the long experience of experts in the Central Council for Physical Recreation had been used in all the early planning. I was soon convinced, as so many are, that at the adolescent stage, the greater physical maturity, sensitivity and physical co-ordination of girls actually places them at an advantage in many ways over the majority of boys of the same age. Certainly any lack of muscular toughness was counterbalanced by enthusiasm at the courses I visited.

During my first visit, members of the Rhowniar staff were still talking about a recent course held away from the school at the island of Skye in Scotland. It had been planned both for the benefit of the staff of the school and of a small group of its ex-students. An enterprising programme had clearly been arranged—some extremely adventurous expeditions with canoes and difficult climbing, together with a community service project planned jointly with a local youth group to build an adventure centre for the young people of Skye. I was not able to judge the value of this new type of extension course for the students who went on it, but the experience had certainly welded the staff of Rhowniar into a strong unity.

On my way to the school at Rhowniar I had paused at Aberdovey for a further talk with Captain Fuller. It was at Aberdovey that the fanciful picture I had formed of a typical Outward Bound warden had been destroyed. If I had had any similar picture of a female warden it would have contained some elements of the character of a hockey captain at St. Trinian's school, but this too would have vanished on a first meeting with Anne Cordiner, so slim, reserved and quietly Scottish was the Rhowniar Warden, notwithstanding that she was particularly well qualified in mountaineering and swimming and an instructor also for the Mountaineering Association of Great Britain.

As I drove back to England from west Wales I reflected on the good fortune of the Outward Bound Trust in being able to attract to the wardenship of their schools, at such a critical time, five men and one woman with such varied backgrounds of experience, so committed to their work and so forward looking.

This selective and personal account of the work of the British schools makes no attempt to give a fair or a balanced picture either of them or their wardens. It is included mainly in order to give a 'local habitation and a name' to each of the standard courses described later. Inevitably my first impression of the schools and their personnel were partial. My purpose on the first round of visits was not so much to understand the schools as to use them in trying to discover what their influence was on past students. It is not immoral to use an institution (or a person) for some purpose that seems to you a good one, but this is not the quickest way to discover its (or his) essential nature.

3. THE SCHOOLS OVERSEAS

A measure of the fundamental truth in a new educational idea is to be found in the degree to which it spreads beyond the borders of its country of origin. I was always surprised, for example, when I met little girl guides in their blue serge tunics in deserts or jungles, looking for all the world as if they were returning from a meeting in the hall of an English village. An experience brought this home to me when I was once trapped between two flooded rivers in southern Uganda. I had just managed to get across one of the rivers and found that a well laden lorry had broken down the only bridge across the second and was firmly sunk in the mud. The crew of the lorry had disappeared so I hoped they had scrambled ashore on the opposite bank and gone to get help. After an hour a Ministry of Transport lorry appeared on the opposite bank with the missing crew and a gang of road workers. After inspecting the situation the gang started to build a fire and to begin a conference, presumably on the subject of possible remedies. No one was in a hurry. It was raining so no one would die of thirst and the banana trees all around were yellow with fruit. After some hours of tranquillity there emerged from a narrow jungle footpath a girl guide, in the well-known uniform, wheeling a barrow in which was a single rock. With difficulty she tipped this into the swamp beside the bridge. In my meditative mood I calculated that if she returned every five minutes with a single rock, in the course of a year or so, a causeway would exist across the river. In fact she did return several times; and then, suddenly, the committee of road workers broke up, its members climbed into their lorry and drove away. After half an hour they returned with a lorry full of rocks, which they tipped into the swamp. This process was repeated so long as the light lasted and all the next day, and on the third day there was a causeway, and I drove across it. Ever since, in the face of a seemingly hopeless situation, I have always taken some action, however apparently silly, and I have remained interested in the export of English educational ideas.

The ideas that resulted in the setting up of six Outward Bound Schools in Great Britain have spread, first to countries of the British Commonwealth, then to Europe, and finally to the U.S.A. The first work overseas was done in 1951 in Nigeria: an Outward Bound course was organized in the sea and mountain environment of Man O'War bay, just north of the Equator in the Cameroons, only 14 miles from the 13,000 feet Cameroon Mountain itself. The story of this early work in Nigeria has already been told by Hilary Tunstall-Behrens in the book edited by David James called *Outward Bound*. Recruits came from all over Nigeria, a link was made with the energetic community development work of the government, and the first courses were very much a combined operation planned by the first Principal, A. Dickson, and the Community Development Officer for the Eastern Region, M. E. R. Chadwick. If the first measure of adaptation of the Outward Bound idea to Nigerian conditions was the stress laid on the element of community service, the second adaptation was one which soon grew to be of prime significance in all Commonwealth Schools—the emphasis on the breaking down of tribal and religious

differences in the interests of national unity. Students at
the Man O'War School comprised Christians and Moslems, Kanuri, Hausa, Yoruba and Ibo, who, in their
small groups, learnt to work together in the facing of
common tasks and common hazards. Perhaps if there
had been twenty Outward Bound Schools in Nigeria,
instead of only one, the recent tragic civil war might never
have started.

The second Outward Bound School in Africa was
founded in 1956 by a Kenya Provincial Education
Officer, R. A. Lake, who was also very anxious to develop
aspects of inter-racial education. The capital costs of the
school were found by twenty-six business firms that were
anxious to sponsor boys to Outward Bound courses and
it also receives substantial financial support from the
Governments of Kenya, Uganda and Tanzania, all of
whom sponsor students. The opportunities for healing
divisions of race, tribe and religion are as great in East
Africa as in Nigeria. Christians and Moslems, Indians,
Europeans and Africans, Kikuyu, Masai and Baganda all
come to the school. There has been no civil war in East
Africa yet but race relations have often been and still are
strained. If there were ten Outward Bound Schools in
East Africa instead of one, racial, tribal and religious
misunderstandings and animosities would be fewer, and
the danger of civil war remote.

The site for the main centre of Outward Bound
operations in East Africa was chosen at Loitokitok, on
the Kenya–Tanganyika border, about 5,500 feet up the
lower slopes of Mount Kilimanjaro. In the final expedition
of the Loitokitok courses the ascent to the crater of Kibo,
at 18,640 feet, makes it one of the most demanding of
expeditions in any Outward Bound School.

The East African School not only organizes mountain
courses at Loitokitok, but also sea courses at various
points on the Kenya coast north of Mombasa. In 1969

the instructors of the school took up to the top of Kilimanjaro a party of totally blind climbers, consisting of
two men from Kenya, three from Uganda and two from
Tanzania.

Before he relinquished the Governorship of Malaysia
in 1954, Sir Gerald Templer opened an Outward Bound
School at Lumut, Perak, only 100 yards from the sands
of the west coast. In this school, as in the schools of West
Africa, and East Africa, the Governor hoped that group
animosities and misunderstandings would be broken
down. He realized that if a united Malaysia was to be
built, Chinese and Malays would have to learn to work
together and this hope for the future would have to be
founded on the outlook of the rising generation. His
hopes have already been realized, for Malaysia today has
more political stability and her economic future is more
assured than most ex-colonial tropical and multi-racial
nations. This contrast between Malaysia and the ter-
ritories of East and West Africa, which are served by
their two Outward Bound Schools, raises in a new form
the way in which Outward Bound educational principles
should be adapted to African conditions. The two forms
of adaptation already mentioned, of the breaking down of
tribal and religious differences liable to erupt into open
violence, and the placing of special stress on community
service, will continue to assist the process of adaptation
but they will not go the whole way. Many of the ex-
colonial countries are entering a new and difficult phase
of development. After independence, early hopes and
aspirations (and also financial reserves) have crumbled.
Two very large problems have appeared. In the 1960s
African governments concentrated resources on the development of factories, government buildings, urban services,
and education for employment in the modern sector of
the economy. But now, without prosperous rural economies to provide expanding markets for manufactured

goods, industrialization in the urban areas is grinding to a halt. At the same time the *per capita* productivity of the rural sector of the economy is often actually declining. Unemployment and the underemployment of skilled man-power in urban areas has begun to reach alarming proportions. The earlier belief that rapid industrialization would supply goods to replace imports and lead to a perpetually rising standard of living has been shattered. But all forms of education in the past have been oriented almost exclusively to the needs of the African towns. So what is needed now is a re-orientation of education, combined with a modernization and transformation of the rural economy.

At the 1970 World Conference of the Society for International Development, speaker after speaker referred to these two paramount needs in the tropical areas of Africa—political stability and a rural transformation. At this conference also it was realized that the formal agencies of higher education were contributing very little to the solution of either of these needs. It may be that a start will be made first by the informal agencies of higher education and in this the Outward Bound Schools could play a part. If they are to do this, the European 'challenges' that play such an important role in the British, American and European Schools may have to be replaced by quite different challenges of an African kind, arising partly out of the nature of African society and partly through the need to produce individuals whose integrity can help to develop greater political stability and give impetus to a transformation of the rural economy. What seems now to be needed in Africa is a new type of course—as radical, in its way, as the City Challenge Course, but with the title, perhaps, of Rural Challenge. The most recently established of the Outward Bound Schools in Africa are those in Rhodesia and Zambia, both in very suitable environments for the development of both City and Rural

Challenge Courses. These two Schools both offer multi-racial courses.

In Australia, New Zealand, and even the economically prosperous island of Hong Kong, Outward Bound Schools have been established in economies that approach more nearly to those of the U.K. and the U.S.A. than those of Africa, so that the way forward for this group of schools should need a less radical degree of adaptation.

The Outward Bound Schools in Great Britain owed a great deal of their inspiration to the work and ideas of Kurt Hahn, the Headmaster of Gordonstoun School at Elgin, and previously Headmaster of Schule Schloss Salem in Germany, who, in 1936, joined forces with the Headmaster of Elgin Academy in Scotland to establish the Moray Badge Scheme, which was the forerunner of the present Duke of Edinburgh's Award Scheme. It was eight years after the end of the war that the educational ideas so tragically destroyed by Hitler at Salem in 1932 began to blossom again on German soil, and then, in June 1953, the President of the Republic of West Germany opened an Outward Bound Sea School on the shores of the Baltic at Weissenhaus, a town already well known in Germany for the high standard of its work in sea and land rescue. Two mountain schools followed, one at Hitler's mountain fastness of Berchtesgaden and the other at Baad in the Black Mountains of Austria. A fourth European school has been opened as a sea school on the Dutch coast and its first complement of staff went for their initial training to the sea school at Aberdovey. This school keeps a few places in its courses for boys from Great Britain and the British Council has also assisted exchange schemes between British and European Schools.

The first Outward Bound School in the U.S.A. was founded in Colorado in 1962 and since then four more have been set up—in Minnesota, Maine, Oregon, and North Carolina. This growth from one to five schools in five years is fast even for the go-getting Americans.

In 1970, Roger Putnam, the Warden of Eskdale School, visited the U.S.A. to study the American schools. His report shows some of the different ways in which the educational principles of Outward Bound have been adapted to the educational, geographical and administrative scene on the other side of the Atlantic. These differences spring partly from the way in which, over the years, the administration of the schools has developed. Each school has its own Board of Directors or Trustees as in Great Britain but these work in greater independence of Outward Bound Incorporated U.S.A. than do the British Boards of Directors of the Central Outward Bound Trust. In the U.S.A. each school is almost wholly responsible for raising its own funds, recruiting its own students, and freely appointing its own staff. This difference is linked with the practice in nearly all schools of running standard courses only in the four summer months of June to September. This has two important results. During the winter months the warden and some of the administrative staff move from their summer quarters to a city to plan new work, to raise funds, to recruit and train staff, and to recruit students. At the same time other full-time instructors, having had special training, go off to work as qualified adventure-training instructors in institutions of the formal educational system. In this way the system has been greatly influenced by Outward Bound ideas and some Americans see the future of Outward Bound work mainly in terms of the training of teachers and the use of trained instructors in schools, colleges and universities. Certainly these winter activities serve the dual purpose of widening the areas in which Outward Bound is known and using a well qualified nucleus of full-time staff over the whole year. As in Great Britain, however, many variations of the standard course have been invented, some particularly suited to the American geographical scene, such as courses in which river-rafting or skiing are the central outdoor skills, and others which provide for special groups like teachers or delinquents.

At most of the American schools a greater emphasis is placed on the 'solo' expedition than is usual at British Schools. This expedition is at least three times as long as the British, and it is less a matter of walking, climbing and camping than an exercise in survival and introspection.

At one school, in the middle of a canoe trip each member of the party is dropped at a different spot and has to live 'on the country' with only a groundsheet, knife, first-aid kit, bug-repellent, flashlight, salt, four matches, four fishhooks and line, a whistle and an orange flag. An apocryphal story from the U.S.A. tells of a girl member of a course who returned to base after three days, very thin and hungry, but carrying a plump, well fed marmot! One feature of the 'solo' expedition that many students claim to be of lasting influence is the requirement placed on the student to keep a careful diary of its 'introspection' aspect.

In most of the American schools, the policy has been one of deliberate decentralization, reducing courses in permanent school buildings. The central site is increasingly used only for special courses, and for the early days of 'basic' training before a course becomes 'mobile' and moves off into wild country, which may sometimes be as far as 100 miles from the school. The wide use of simultaneous mobile courses means that a school can organize courses for as many as 1,000 students in the June to September period. This decentralized form of operation requires great administrative ability in the central staff and high teaching ability in the leaders of each patrol.

The main aim of the visit of Roger Putnam was to

study the American concept of the mobile course, and to establish in what ways it might be used in Great Britain. In his report, he mentions, among other advantages, the fact that students within a patrol relate to each other more effectively than at a standard course, since there is continuous and total involvement with the course dictated by common isolation and hardships. By this means group identity is fostered and group cohesion strengthened. The involvement of an instructor is equally deep and his relationship with the members of his patrol is closer and more effective than when he is felt to be a member of a central school staff. In mobile courses the exercises and challenges are less contrived and so more realistic than on a central course and the changing daily scene gives tremendous scope for flexibility in the organization of the programme and particular situations as they arise are exploited to the full. This variety and freedom in the programme and the degree of independence and initiative it gives them make it highly attractive to instructors, who are in no danger of getting 'stale' as one course succeeds another. Finally, Roger Putnam noted that the small use of a central school meant that capital expenditure on buildings and plant was minimized and funds could be used for providing really high quality personal equipment to the mobile patrols.

The limitations of a mobile course were also appreciated in Roger Putnam's report. It is particularly susceptible to long periods of bad weather. It places great responsibility and thereby strain on patrol instructors, who may be alone with their patrols for days at a time without the opportunity to turn to other instructors for advice or assistance. The members of a patrol do not, in such a situation, get the advantages of team instruction. It is difficult also to cope with minor casualties since mobile courses generally operate in remote regions where medical and reserve services are distant and limited.

Roger Putnam concluded his report with the following words: 'there is no question in my mind that provided the calibre of Staff is right, the Mobile Course is a highly effective scheme for the development of self-discipline, responsibility and compassion in young people'.

4. STANDARD COURSES

The prospectus of one of the schools describes the aims of the Standard Course Training as follows:

'The standard training aims for self-discovery through experience. The programme is not a "Commando Course"; it is designed to be a mentally and physically stimulating month containing a challenge for every student. Attitude is stressed more than strength; mental stamina more than skill. The programme is finely balanced between the needs of a varied and unusual set of physical and mental challenges.'

The daily programme for this school (and it is typical of all the schools) which gives effect to these aims, is given overleaf.

This is the programme of activities with which each student is presented before he arrives and which is explained at the briefing session on the first day. It is surprising how rarely schoolmasters take their pupils into their confidence in this way. In some schools there are still severe punishments for idleness and bad or slow work, yet in these schools especially, though pupils are spoon-fed, they can never see the way ahead nor are able to relate one day's work or one hour's work to the next and to the whole plan of learning progress. It is not surprising that co-operation is not given to some teachers when purposes and objectives and stages of the process

Day	Morning	Afternoon	Evening
1	Medical Examination—Tolerance Tests, Interviews	Map Reading, Knots, Artificial Respiration	First Aid Training Film
2	Basic Canoeing 1	Lifesaving, Fitness Training, Campcraft, Rope Handling	Informal Discussions with Patrol Instructor
3	Surf Lifesaving Training	Briefing and Preparation	Depart on 'Shakedown'
4	Expedition—Navigation, Group Leadership, Campcraft		
5	Route Planning, Ecology and Rock Climbing		Cleaning equipment, de-briefing
6	Swimming—Lifesaving, First Aid, Agility Course	Basic Canoeing 11	Lecture: Use of Leisure
7	Voluntary Church, Free	Volleyball Competition, Emergencies	Self Expression
8	Map Reading, First Aid Movement to Music	High Ropes, Agility and Confidence Test	Free
9	Aqualung Training	Drama, First Aid, Steeplechase	Briefing and Preparation
10 11	Roving Expedition—Canoeing or Sailing, Climbing, Camping, Walking		
12			Cleaning equipment, de-briefing
13	Swimming, Movement to Music	Orienteering, Staff Conference	Mid-course Interviews
14	Voluntary Church, Free	Beach Patrol, Belt and Reel Surf Training, Canoeing	Free or Film
15	Wall and Beam, First Aid, Swimming	Estate Work	Debate Preparation
16	Cave Expedition and Survey		Individual Lecturettes
17	Drama, First Aid	Aqualung Training	Lecture

DAY	MORNING	AFTERNOON	EVENING
18	Berry Head—Operating from Coastguard Station		
19	Cliff Evacuation—Breeches Buoy, Abseiling		
20	Beach Patrol—Surf Canoeing, Belt and Reel Training		Debate
21	Voluntary Church, Free	Choice of Activity, Volleyball	Free or Film
22	Devon or Cornwall 'Overland' Expedition		
23	Unaccompanied groups of 4 from coast to coast		
24	Sustained effort, Planning, Leadership,		
25	Teamwork		Formal debriefing
26	Warden, Doctor, Course Impressions, Hand in equipment	Devon Pentathalon	Badge presentation, Concert
	DEPART		

of acquiring skills and knowledge are never put before pupils. When they are well briefed and can see how each week's work and progress fits into the programme for a term and how each term fits into the plan for a year, their desire to learn is very greatly increased, in my experience, and punishments for slackness in work never needed.

On the first day the time devoted to briefing and to individual interviews will include a discussion of what are called the Training Conditions which all students are asked to observe during the course. Over the last few years there has been no more controversial subject for discussion among wardens and their staffs than this. In the early years there was a firm rule that no smoking or drinking were to be permitted for the duration of the course. On the physical side, courses are demanding and it was held that much of the work would be wasted and the course not really enjoyed by a student whose smoking and drinking habits left him only half-fit. Until the Ullswater Conference of Wardens and Senior Staff in 1967, failure to keep this rule resulted in the loss of the Outward Bound Badge awarded at the end of the course. Since that conference it has been decided to keep the training conditions but to relate them much more to the general encouragement of self-discipline.

If a student loses his temper and hits another or if a student cuts his morning dip, which he may hate or even fear, his group-instructor will do all he can to help him cure some weakness in his character. If a student is discovered smoking, the same principle applies. If he is an addict and has been in the habit of smoking some thirty or forty cigarettes a day, the urge to smoke may be very great. His group-instructor, and the warden if it comes to his notice, can help him to fight what is a very real temptation. Mid-course interviews often reveal failures of this kind. Only then can the group-instructor gain the confidence of the student and be enabled to help and encourage—and go on helping and encouraging—him to conquer his weakness or lack of will-power. If, however, the student is obviously making no effort to observe training conditions and could not care less, then it is perfectly justifiable to point out to him that his attitude will only result in his being deprived of his badge.

The programme for a standard course contains certain elements that are common to the programmes of all Outward Bound Schools, elements that long experience has shown to be of particular value. In addition there are elements which differ from school to school, depending on the particular facilities which the region round the school affords, and also the particular kinds of expertise which the staff of a school possesses. Martin Hardcastle in his 1969 report distinguished between these two elements and his brief descriptions are used here as a way of supplementing the programme of a standard course given above. The common elements in all courses may be listed as follows:

1. Canoeing

Students learn about the construction of canoes and help in the canoe-building shop. Many students go on to build their own canoes after leaving a course. The particular value of canoeing lies in the fact that the necessary degree of skill can be learnt quickly and then this most enjoyable and healthy activity is within the means of all young workers. It takes them into unspoilt country and away from the crowded roads. Capsize drill can be learnt in the swimming pool as can also the more advanced skill of 'canoe-rolling'. Some schools have outdoor heated swimming pools and it is the aim to equip all schools in this way so that instructors can stand in water for a considerable period of time while instructing on canoeing.

2. Swimming

Non-swimmers are taught to swim and swimmers to improve their skills. Two other skills related to sea and lake rescue are taught: these are 'survival swimming' or the skill of moving through the water over a long distance with the minimum expenditure of energy; and 'drown-proofing', or the skill of remaining afloat in a vertical position, while only moving the head rhythmically in order to take in air. This latter skill is difficult to learn in the early stages and depends very much on expert instruction and the confidence which instructors can pass on to those without it.

3. Rock-climbing

The mountain schools have very good climbing facilities close at hand but all the schools have suitable rock slopes within easy range. Some of the descents of vertical or overhanging falls by the 'abseil' method are spectacular and must seem terrifying to the uninitiated, but they are absolutely safe, as all students soon learn. Although the majority of the girl students at Rhowniar regard climbing at the outset with some misgiving, about three-quarters leave with the firm intention of continuing to climb and it is, in fact, the activity with the strongest follow-up.

4. The wall, beam, and high ropes

In all schools athletic agility is developed by the 'commando-type' apparatus of the climbing wall and beam, and by an ingenious arrangement of fixed and swinging ropes knotted from tree to tree in a woodland clearing. This apparatus lends itself to the excitement of group competitions and is an early way of developing mutual assistance among the members of a group.

The high ropes provide for some the greatest challenge on the course; they certainly look formidable and to the nervous student must present an extremely unattractive prospect, though the Tarzan-like derive enormous fun from them. The important point is that no one is dragooned into going round the ropes course nor made to feel that failure is shameful. The instructors give the weaker students every encouragement, and it is noticeable how the rest of the group help and encourage them, too, so that even if the weaker ones do not complete the course successfully they are made to feel that a really stout effort is what matters, even if it fails. Real success lies in what the nervous and weak achieve over and above what they think they can do. Thus is self-confidence developed. The rope courses are potentially dangerous, but the danger is reduced to a justifiable minimum by the fact that safety devices are insisted upon for any item on the circuit for which the student's legs are more than a few feet above the ground. This is a common policy agreed by the wardens.

5. Expeditions

At all schools one of the main challenges of the course is the three- (or four-) day expedition, when the students are on their own in the hills or mountains and to a large extent plan their own route. At most schools, indeed, this expedition forms the climax of the course, though at the sea schools, where nautical training is a main factor, the expedition provides one of the peaks of the course, but not the climax.

In every case the training for these expeditions is very thorough. Previous instruction in and practical experience of map-reading and first aid play a very essential part. Programmes naturally vary somewhat, but a typical example is as follows: a one-day expedition for each group with an instructor; later a three- or four-day expedition with instructors after combining with other groups at camps or huts. The group generally make their way to and from the camps on their own. Rock-climbing, canoeing, or forestry are included in the programme whenever the route makes these possible. Some schools also have a single-day expedition in the hills or mountains without an instructor.

The briefing for the 'final' expedition is as impressively thorough as are the preliminary instruction and training experience. All this justifies the calculated risk that is taken in allowing boys (or girls) to set out on their own in mountainous or remote moorland country. The general practice is for the whole course to be briefed by the chief instructor; for the student leaders (who shoulder more responsibility during the expedition than at any other time during the course) to be briefed by the Warden;

and for the different groups to be briefed by their group-instructors.

On any expedition a group (usually from four to six in number) may be faced with some minor crisis—a sprained ankle, a case of exhaustion, losing their route in cloud conditions, etc; and then they know exactly what to do, and their efficiency and good sense on these occasions indicate the value of their careful and thorough training. Indeed the ability of these young people (who often have never seen a mountain before the course) to cope with challenging conditions and unexpected emergencies is one of the outstanding features of the training.

There are, of course, numerous instructors out in the area, either unobtrusively moving round or at fixed bases known to the groups, which are therefore never far away from help.

The Rhowniar three-day final expedition takes place in wild and remote country with numerous hills and lesser mountains, but less rugged and easier for the instructors to control. The loads carried are naturally somewhat lighter than for the boys and the parties converge on pre-arranged camp-sites in the evening, where instructors are based and tents ready to be pitched. But the challenge of planning their route, of finding their way and of stretching themselves to the limit is no less for the girls than for the boys.

At some schools a 'solo' expedition is an important item in the course. Each boy carries a bivouac-type tent and all the necessities for a one-night camp. He is given a map reference for the place at which he is to camp. It is not far from the school, but he makes his way alone by a devious set route. The boy is entirely on his own and dependent on himself, except that the group-instructor visits him in the evening to see how he is faring. Some are entirely self-reliant and competent; but others make the most elementary mistakes (usually because they have not really believed it necessary to carry out their instructions!) They learn from experience, bitter though it sometimes is, and profit by their mistakes. This is of considerable value later on in the final expedition.

The expeditions are all useful, but for some the solo expedition is an outstanding experience. Course 'impressions' testify to this, especially in the case of those who come from cities and have never known what it is to be alone; all their lives they have depended on someone else. Quite a number are scared by the silence and the loneliness, which can constitute a greater challenge than anything else on the course.

6. Orienteering

This has recently become an item in nearly every school's programme. Carried out in pairs or threes in mountainous or wooded country according to the terrain available, it provides excellent practical experience in map-reading and a physical challenge as well.

7. Sea and mountain rescue training

At all schools there is cliff rescue training with stretcher lowering and carrying practice. At the sea and mountain schools there are recognized and accredited sea and mountain rescue units. In a search large numbers of boys are often used. Sometimes rescue calls prove abortive— lost persons turn up safe and sound elsewhere or another rescue party has arrived first—but the rescue log-books in the various schools show that invaluable practical assistance has time and again been rendered and lives saved by prompt and efficient action. The response of the students is remarkable, and would surprise many who decry the qualities of the modern generation. Although rescue teams are always led by instructors, it is not uncommon for a group on an expedition to come across an accident or emergency of some kind and to cope with the situation responsibly and effectively without any assistance from instructors.

8. Cultural and Intellectual Activities

There is a considerable variety of cultural activities in all schools, though some have gone further in this direction than others. Discussions on a wide variety of subjects, public-speaking in the form of lecturettes and illustrated talks by visiting lecturers are common to all schools. Some schools concentrate on project work that arises out of or is related to expeditions. There is no doubt that mere footslogging expeditions across moors and fells have little appeal for the majority of young people. Many students do not see much point in them except as training in toughness, and derive little pleasure or interest from them, especially if the weather is adverse, though they may have a considerable sense of achievement at the end. For this reason an expedition with a project in view gives a stimulus and extra incentive to the more intelligent and it may well provide some who are not so good at the physical activities with the chance of making some positive contribution to the success of their group. This is why project work is being developed in the schools. There is a wide field of possible projects in field-studies: in geology, animal life, local history, antiquities, ancient roads, the development of farming, etc., and each school has varied possibilities in its own locality.

In the school programme quoted at the beginning of this chapter music and drama sessions are mentioned and these or other creative activities have been used in several schools.

9. Reports

After every activity during the course the instructor
responsible for the activity writes some comment on each
student in a book which the group-instructor keeps for
the purpose. This helps to build up a picture of the
student, his abilities and his character, which greatly
assists the instructor in writing an end-of-course report
on each of the students in his group in considerable detail.
A heavy burden of responsibility is imposed on those who
produce these final reports, and they fully appreciate this.
Certainly no pains are spared to give a true impression
of the boy or girl concerned and sponsors rate the quality
of these reports very highly.

10. Interviews

It is the general custom for the group-instructor to interview his or her students half-way through the course and
again at the end. 'Interview' is perhaps a misleading term,
for there is nothing formal about it; it takes the form of a
frank and friendly talk at which the student can speak as
freely as the instructor. These interviews help many of
the students to overcome weaknesses and to develop
increasing confidence. An end-of-course interview is of
no less value; it helps the student to know himself and to
be better equipped for his return to his normal life. In
some cases it is not too much to say that no one in his life
has known a student as well as the group-instructor does
by the end of the course. Obviously the value of the
interview varies with the quality and experience of the
instructors, but course impressions by students are full
of tributes to their friendship and to the influence of the
interviews.

11. Course Impressions

At most schools students are given about an hour to write their course impressions on the last day of the course. To avoid waste of time in lengthy descriptions of particular activities, various points are suggested for them to write on; for junior courses specific headings are often given. They are asked to write freely and frankly. It has been argued that there is a certain atmosphere of euphoria at the end of a course and so the students are inclined to view it through somewhat rosy spectacles. Whether this is so or not, there are generally critical comments, though, in the main, there is deep appreciation. Certainly these 'impressions' are immensely interesting and rewarding to read. They give the student a chance to pause and think what he has got out of the course; they often let the warden know that difficult students have derived more benefit from the course than they had thought possible; they sometimes reveal unsuspected weaknesses in programme or organization; and they sometimes enable the warden to note some unrealized weakness in an instructor.

12. Religion

All schools have 'family prayers' in the morning, where there is a short reading. In some cases instructors, in others students, are responsible for choosing and delivering these readings. They are usually not of an obviously 'religious' nature. The most effective are those which bring home some moral but practical point relating to the course, e.g. courage, unselfishness, mutual trust, humility, tolerance, sympathy, loneliness, or cheerfulness. Some schools have compiled their own anthology of readings which instructors find useful.

In the matter of Sunday observances there is considerable diversity in the schools. This is inevitable, for some are far removed from any place of worship while others have a variety fairly close at hand. Two schools have small chapels of their own. One or two are fortunate in having a local parson who is genuinely interested in the school, who has a flair for dealing with young people, and who is invited to visit the school and to take part in evening discussions. At all schools church attendance is quite voluntary but every facility is provided for those who choose to attend.

In several schools a most valuable and impressive feature is the 'discussion' period which takes place in the evening, usually, but not necessarily, on a Sunday. The word 'religious' is not applied to these as a rule, but in fact all sorts of issues—religious, moral, human—are brought up. Normally the whole course attends; the variety of questions and the interest shown are very striking. It is seldom that discussion hangs fire and often argument continues long afterwards in the dormitories! Much depends on the chairman of the panel which guides the discussion and endeavours to answer the questions. Often the warden presides, but visitors from outside are frequently invited. One particularly successful example will serve to illustrate the value of these 'discussions'.

At Moray recently three priests—Episcopalian, Roman Catholic and the local Presbyterian minister—were at the receiving end of a non-stop bombardment of challenging questions for over an hour. Their frank and sincere replies, representing quite different points of view, created deep and genuine interest among the great majority of students, revealing that there are many young people, averse though they may be to organized religion, who are deeply concerned with the human problems of today.

13. Community Service

In addition to the sea and mountain rescue organization already mentioned each school endeavours to find ways

C.O.B.—3

of helping the local community. The girls of Rhowniar
give practical help in the homes of elderly people in the
neighbouring towns. At the boys' schools practical assistance is given to farmers, the Forestry Commission or the
National Trust, often involving heavy and tedious work,
as for instance in the carrying of fencing up mountain
sides or in the rescue of sheep—no uncommon occurrence!
This help is generally appreciated, though cases are not
unknown when the school concerned has not received a
word of thanks! It is given unobtrusively, the schools
make light of it, and I had to be quite determined in my
inquiries to find out much about it. This is as it should be,
but the wardens and staff of schools were in no doubt
about the importance of this thread of service in the
programme of every course.

5. TESTING THE STANDARD COURSE

As soon as I had finished my first tour to all the Outward Bound Schools I began to devise the statistical inquiry which I hoped would reveal both the strengths and the weaknesses of the standard course; and also the degree to which a standard course met the rather different aims and needs of the students and of their sponsors (who, I supposed, might have aims and needs rather different from those of the students).

In devising this study I was helped by two earlier follow-up studies carried out with groups of Outward Bound students in 1958 and 1965.

In 1958 a postgraduate research student at Oxford had carried out a study by questionnaire and interview of ex-students of Outward Bound Schools. The schools have changed since 1958 but it is worthy of note that P. Carpenter, who carried out the Oxford study, summarized his findings as revealing four major advantages mentioned by all but a small minority of students: (i) an all-round improvement in physical fitness, (ii) a great increase in self-confidence, (iii) an acceleration of the growing-up process, and (iv) an increase in the ability to face and overcome problems and difficult situations.

A second follow-up study of students was carried out by Richard Tosswill of the Distington Engineering Co. Ltd in Cumberland. In 1964, Tosswill had worked as an instructor for a time at the Eskdale Mountain School. During 1964 he was the patrol instructor of a patrol in ten successive courses, which meant that he came to know about 100 students very well as individuals. He waited until they had been away from the school for two years and then sent them a lengthy questionnaire designed to secure their views of the course they had attended and the degree of its influence on their subsequent life. He put no limit to the length of replies so that some students wrote long but very illuminating answers to his questions. Only sixty-six or two-thirds of his students replied to his inquiry but this is a little higher than the normal 60 per cent return for a questionnaire inquiry and particularly high for a group in the 18–22 age bracket; no doubt his personal letters and (as emerged from the replies) the fact that he was a much liked and respected instructor greatly helped.

Unfortunately the volume of evidence from this postal inquiry was so bulky that a busy officer of an industrial organization was not able to find the time to analyse it. In 1968 Mr. Tosswill kindly sent it all on to me and I found the time spent on it rewarding because it helped me design a questionnaire based on the major lines of evidence emerging naturally from a wide-ranging inquiry.

In addition to the results of the Tosswill inquiry and before devising my own questionnaires to be sent to students and their sponsors I read carefully the abstracts I had made from the reading of some 500 'Impressions of the Course' which this number of students had written on the final or penultimate days of their courses. I realized that course impressions, while they had the great merit of freshness and immediacy, had the defect that they were written so close to immediate events that a considered judgement was not possible. On the other hand, the views expressed by Mr. Tosswill's students were the result of a two-year period of reflection and had the greater maturity that two years adds to an individual in adolescence. Together, these two groups of estimates of Outward Bound Courses enabled me to devise a questionnaire which I then submitted to university colleagues for criticism.

The value of any follow-up study by a questionnaire method is very largely proportional to the care taken in the selection of questions. They must be unambiguous. They must not reflect the views of the questioner. They must never be leading questions. Most must be capable of short simple answers so that the results of individual sets of replies can be compared and analysed. They must cover the whole field of inquiry, not just sections of it. Finally, they must include a certain number of questions that are open-ended and allow freedom to the individual questioned. For all these reasons it is desirable to test the questionnaire with a limited group, to analyse the answers and in the light of this experience to rephrase it if necessary. I decided to carry out this pilot study with a group of past students of the Devon School in order that I might have the useful co-operation of its warden and his staff. Its nearness to the University of Bristol made many visits to the school possible so that the results of a postal survey could be checked by interviews with past students of the school. In this pilot study eighty students or a 10 per cent random sample of the 800 students attending courses during the 1968 session were selected for study. The selection was a random one, ten students from each of the eight groups described below:

(*a*) Students selected by the warden as being typical of the best students of the year.

(*b*) Students selected by the warden as being typical of the worst students of the year or even complete failures.

(*c*) Those sent by the Home Office.

(*d*) Those seconded by army, navy or air force.

(*e*) Those seconded by the police or the fire service.
(*f*) Those sponsored by industry.
(*g*) Those sponsored by banking and commerce.
(*h*) Those sponsored by parents, schools, L.E.A.s or private associations.

The questionnaires were despatched in February 1969 and most replies had been received by the end of March. There were sixty-one sponsors of the eighty students and fifty, or 82 per cent, of these replied, while fifty-eight, or 72 per cent, students replied. These percentages for the returns are high, since most questionnaires yield only a 60 per cent return or even less.

After the replies from students and sponsors had been analysed, both questionnaires were redesigned for use with the much larger population of approximately 3,000 students and their sponsors who had followed (or sponsored students to) courses at any of the six schools in 1968. In this larger survey replies were received from 87 per cent of sponsors and 78 per cent of students. These very high figures must be due to the fact that most of the questionnaires were sent with an accompanying letter signed by a warden (often with a personal note). Approximately 10 per cent of letters to students were returned because of change of address but there was not sufficient time available to follow these students up. Another 10 per cent of questionnaires were returned with a lengthy amplifying statement of views.

The first part of the inquiry concerned recruitment to the courses. Since one of its aims is to improve the ability of each student to mix well with others of the same age but with very different backgrounds and outlook it is essential that each group of 100 students making up a course should be of as varied a character as possible. The achievement of this aim alone would put Outward Bound education in a different category from all other forms of democractic education in Britain today, for, in spite of the extension and democratization of secondary and higher education, all sociological studies show that the home is still an immensely powerful influence on boys and girls during their schooldays. The percentage of children of manual workers who are able to reach any form of higher education is still tiny, little larger than it was fifty years ago.

The objective of securing a very varied student group is partially achieved by recruiting from the six very different categories already mentioned. These may be set out in the following contrasted pairs:

1. Those sponsored by parents, schools, local education authorities or private associations. This group contains a high proportion of intelligent sixth-form boys and girls expecting to go on to some form of higher education and coming from good homes; and

1a. Those sponsored by the Home Office from boys and girls at Home Office schools, detention centres or under probationary care. This group contains a high proportion of those who have been failures at school, who come from broken homes or have suffered from inadequate parental care, and who are frequently of low intelligence.

2. Those sponsored by industry, and generally enrolled by an apprenticeship scheme or attending courses in further education; and

2a. Those sponsored by banks or commercial houses or light industry.

3. Those seconded by the army, navy or air force and so coming from a highly disciplined system of training; and

3a. Those seconded by the police, the fire service or the merchant navy, with experience of a different kind of discipline from that of the armed services.

In addition to this six-fold variety of recruitment an

additional variation arises from the very different motives in the minds of individual sponsors within any one of the categories. For example, some industrial sponsors award a place at a school as a reward for exceptionally good service to the firm. Others deliberately select near-failures in the hope that a course may save them from dismissal. Between these two extremes all kinds of motives are quoted as influencing sponsors. Nevertheless the inquiry showed that there was a measure of agreement in three fields. About 80 per cent of all sponsors said that they sent students to the schools in order to produce an all-round development of character, whilst 40 per cent spoke of their more specific hopes that a course would either develop leadership qualities or develop the ability to work with people of all kinds or both.

Whatever the sponsors' objectives, 98·5 per cent reported a high or moderate degree of success in their achievement. So only 1·5 per cent of students sent on courses disappointed their sponsors. These figures agreed very well with the views of students, since only 1 per cent reported that the course had been a failure for them.

A different way of measuring the recruits' variety of attitudes towards the courses is found by asking them whether they came under any pressure from sponsors, if they came readily, or if they were eager to come and had themselves sought an invitation. Only 4 per cent of the large sample came under pressure and as many as 60 per cent reported their keenness to participate in a course.

So far as previous experience of the kind of outdoor pursuits of the schools is concerned, 36 per cent of the large sample reported that they had had little experience of such pursuits before coming on a course, 40 per cent reported that they had had some experience or some interest in such pursuits, and a 24 per cent minority expressed a keen interest in and previous experience of one or more of such activities.

The central section of the large group inquiry was aimed at discovering students' views of the 'quality' of five selected aspects of the course and the 'importance' to them personally of ten aspects of the course. It is interesting to see the order in which majority opinion placed these fifteen comparative selections.

So far as quality is concerned the highest grading was given to the teaching provided by the school and very high gradings were given to the amount and quality of the school's equipment and to its excellent organization of outdoor pursuits. The importance to the individual student of the selected ten aspects of the course produced the following order of ranking:

1. A sense of improved physical fitness and of euphoria by the end of the course.
2. The improved ability to face situations of hazard and to overcome problems and difficulties.
3. The improved ability to mix with people of all types and to have increased tolerance for their points of view.
4. The improvement in or the learning of a new outdoor skill.
5. The better understanding of the way in which a small group or team works successfully.
6. A new appreciation of the beauty of the countryside and of the need to conserve its natural resources.
7. Individual help given personally by one or other of the instructors of the school.
8. The value of the discipline of giving up smoking and drinking.
9. The opportunity to participate in rescue activities and community service.
10. The enjoyment of intellectual and cultural activities provided during the course.

Each one of these selected aspects was given the highest

grading by some students but an analysis of all gradings
produced the ranking order shown. In addition to the
reaction of individuals to a course there was a good deal
of evidence that the sub-groups into which a course is
divided develop a strong group life as the course proceeds
and then come to have a group-reaction to the course. In
order to follow this up a little further the views of the
personnel of the eight groups or 'watches' into which a
course at the Moray School is divided was made the
object of a special study. It was clear that all the groups
were able to distinguish between their enjoyment of some
chosen aspect of the course and their assessment of the
value and importance to them of that aspect. When asked,
each of seven groups (of approximately twelve members
each) was able to express a unanimous or almost unanimous
preference for some particular aspect from the point of
view of enjoyment and then of importance.

The results of this study of group reactions revealed
strong group differences. No one group chose the same
combination of enjoyment and importance as any other
group. Most of the groups came to think that the physical
education aspect of the course was the most important
but this must reflect in some degree the interest and
expertise of the warden of the school. However, this was
not quite unanimous and the groups varied particularly
in their selection of the most enjoyable aspect.

This variety of reaction among the sub-groups is a
rough measure of the efficacy of the group training of the
school. The last decade has produced a good deal of
literature on the value of group activity in education,
but the value of this type of work has never been
better expressed than it was fifty years ago by William
McDougall at Cambridge:

'It is the peculiar merit of the complex motives that
arise in the expression of the group spirit that they bring
the self-seeking impulses into the service of a larger

society and harmonize them with the altruistic impulses so that instead of being in conflict these reinforce each other. The development of a sentiment of attachment to one group not only does not prevent, but rather facilitates the development of similar sentiments for other groups. This is especially true when the groups are related to one another as parts and wholes.'

In some of the new experimental courses held at Outward Bound Schools, the total numbers in a course may for special reasons be kept as low as twenty. Even so, such a group will be divided into two sub-groups of ten for most of the activities of the course and this is a measure of the value wardens and instructors have come to put on the group system of education.

6. DEVELOPMENT

Once the standard course had become established and well known, wardens began to think of varying the normal pattern. The first experiments were modest variations in the ages of the participants. The age range of the standard course, 16–19 years, was the obvious one with which to begin, since the three years after leaving school are vital in adolescent education. However, there were some teachers and officers of local education authorities who could secure the release in term-time of pupils in the 14–16 range and who thought that a course might be of educational value, particularly for children in city schools, since its concentrated experience could be followed up by teachers back in ordinary school. The idea also appealed to the Outward Bound Trust because the recruitment to courses in term-time is less than during school vacations. A number of new junior courses were, therefore, tried out at the Aberdovey and Ullswater Schools, and from these developed a new type of junior course programme that was not just a watered-down form of the standard course but contained different forms of practical outdoor skills combined with a larger measure of project and drama work.

Junior Courses

Junior courses have now spread from Aberdovey and Ullswater to other schools, and their staffs find that because they are different they come as a refreshing change from a solid diet of standard courses; they demand more energy and more patience from the staff, since sometimes members of a course return completely exhausted from an exercise and seem capable of nothing but lying flat on their backs. They revive, however, with remarkable rapidity and are soon rushing about again with abundant energy and spirits.

In adopting the well tried standard course to the needs of schoolboys the wardens and staffs of schools had to retrain themselves for what looked like a mere modification of their past work but which, in the event, proved to be an assignment of a very different kind. Standard courses are designed for young adults, little short of their full physical development, who have already cut the umbilical cord that tied them to the warmth and protection of home and school. In early adolescence, however, the situation is very different. Schoolboys turn rapidly from moods of selfishness to altruism, from bouts of energetic endurance to idle lassitude, from deep absorption in a task to extreme boredom, from self-absorption to gregariousness, and from priggishness to amorality. This is the psychology that had to be related to a course founded on an adult pattern of self-discipline, self-reliance, team-work, endurance up to the limit, and service to others.

Some of the modifications made to the standard course were the natural result of assets which the junior groups themselves bring to their courses. Excited by the prospects of a four-week adventure course in a boarding school they bring great initial enthusiasm in contrast to the attitude of older boys, who have worked a year or two in industry and have often learned to put on an armour of cynicism, and sometimes come with a serious degree of infection with the adult diseases of selfishness and apathy.

The young schoolboys who came to the first courses (and later the schoolgirls) were generally much fitter than the average industrial apprentice. They were used to games and physical education and had not yet degenerated into mere spectators. The physical demands of a course could, therefore, be made more demanding in some ways even if much less in others.

The recruits to junior courses, although young, are not juniors but seniors in their schools. They are in the higher classes and most of them are used to exercising responsibility over more junior boys. The young apprentice, or bank clerk, or police cadet is in the quite different situation of being once again a beginner in a new environment, with few responsibilities. His sense of responsibility needs to be revived, but this is rarely true of the older schoolboy, so that the self-governing nature of Outward Bound courses takes on a different complexion in junior courses.

The recruits to junior courses arrive very familiar with project work and the combination of geographical and natural history pursuits that are included in the study of the environment of a Standard Course. So they take readily to the more narrowly educational activities of a course because these are familiar studies even if pursued now in a much wider and more adventurous setting.

All these special characteristics of a junior course call for the kind of expertise possessed by the good school-teacher. I was anxious to discover the formal qualification of the staffs of all the schools for this special kind of adolescent education and my detailed survey revealed that rather more than half the staff had both a professional qualification in and a period of experience of school-teaching in addition to their specialist qualifications. In their retraining of staff, therefore, the wardens of the schools started with the task half done.

Senior Courses

Somewhat different demands were made on the staff of schools as soon as they began to experiment with senior courses for students of nineteen and over. If a school is prepared to take a student of thirty or so, as some are, he will be older than most of the instructors. The approach of such students to a course is more critical; they want to know why things are done in a particular way; or they are less interested in the value of the course to them personally than in its value and techniques to the youth group or trainees with whom they will be working in the future.

In senior courses of this kind it is possible to emphasize some aspects of a standard course which, while important, cannot be given a central importance. One of these is the idea of community service. This is a sophisticated adult idea much more appropriate to the older man than to those of sixteen to nineteen, when a young adolescent is breaking the ties and obligations of childhood but has not yet assumed the responsibilities and fixity of adult life. He is and must be expected to be less responsible than at any other period of his life.

An example of the way in which community service and rescue activities were given great importance could have been seen at a summer course held at Ullswater Mountain School in 1968.

During the period of this course, a national marathon sailing race had been organized in Lake Ullswater, and while the race was going on, pairs of boys from Ullswater School maintained two-hour watches from dusk to dawn at a camp at the head of the lake and at a watch-tower lower down on its shore. Both rescue points were in touch throughout the night by radio with a central operations room at the school.

This school also maintains an official mountain rescue

post and is equipped with modern rescue devices, walkie-talkie outfits, and a rescue-helicopter landing strip. The way in which this rescue post was operated during the period of one summer course is described by the school warden in his course report:

'On the afternoon of the third Monday of our Summer Course, a call came in from the Police to go to the aid of 12 approved schoolboys and two masters. They were suffering from food poisoning in the High Cup Nick area of the Pennines, where we had been involved on a previous large-scale rescue episode last March.

'Whymper, which was the Duty Mountain Rescue Patrol, was away in very quick time and buses were ordered to take the remainder of the school on what looked like being a large-scale evacuation. We were just about to leave when we heard that the Durham Police had got the whole party down to the Teesdale area and that our services were not required. Ralph Hetherington, with Whymper Patrol, was eventually stopped by a mobile policeman at the bottom of Hartside Pass on their way to Teesdale.

'The next day, after nearly all had left for the rock-climbing expedition, we were asked by Keswick to stand by in support of a search for a missing geology student who was thought to be in trouble down a disused mine, north of Skiddaw in the Northern Fells. After alerting an R.A.F. helicopter from Acklington we stood by all day ready to bring everyone back from the expedition. Fortunately it was found to be a false alarm as the young man was safe in his lodgings and had not thought of telling anybody that he had changed his plans.

'Within an hour another call came in to search for a fourteen-year-old boy missing on the Whiteside flank of Helvellyn. The Patterdale, Keswick and Kendal teams searched for him throughout the night without success so

1. Mixed Course—Northwest Outward Bound School, Oregon.

2. Expedition Planning—Colorado.

3. A group of students climbing to the summit of Kilimanjaro on Final Expedition—Kenya School.

4. Mexican Project, building a school for Indian children carried out by students from Colorado.

5. Canoeing at the Singapore School.

6. Baad, returning home after the expedition.

7. A girls' course from Berchtesgaden walking through the Bavarian Mountains.

8. Sea Rescue Training at the German School on the Baltic—Weissenhaus.

9. Briefing for Mountain Rescue Operation in the Lake District.

10. The Moray Lifeboat.

11. Freddy Fuller, late Warden of Aberdovey, talks to German boys on an exchange visit.

12. Junior Students working in the project room at Ullswater.

13. Boys engage on a home-help project.

14. Helping at a play centre.

15. Youth helping old age.

16. Cutter returning to Harbour at Burghead.

17. Getting the hang of it!—Aberdovey.

18. The first Mixed Course.

19. New Discoveries—Girls' Course.

20. The Schools located in places of great beauty—The Girls' School, Wales.

21. The new Summers Wing at Moray.

22. Climbing in the Lake District—Students from Eskdale.

23. A Junior Course climbing through Styhead Pass in the Scafell range—Students from Ullswater.

24. Agility training at Eskdale School.

25. Canoeing on the River Dart—Devon School.

26. Surf canoeing—The South Devon Coast.

we set up the mobile operations board in the Patterdale Rescue Post at Deerhow, Patterdale, at 0700 hours on the Wednesday morning. Dr. Ogilvie was the Search Controller, and the Lake District Mountain Rescue Panel was called in two hours later to organize a large-scale research operation.

'Half of our students were unobtainable as they were still walking out to the camp-sites on the Walna Scar Road below Dow Crag, Seathwaite and Borrowdale and to a new climbing area for us in upper Deepdale. However, we were able to bring the other half away from those camp-sites—it meant that they missed their rock-climbing for that day—to join the search parties. Altogether 34 search parties from most of the mountain rescue teams of Lakeland as well as others from as far afield as Yorkshire and Stafford were involved and it developed into the largest one-day search, totalling over 420 people, ever known in these mountains. In the event it was all un-necessary and was another example of the irresponsibility and stupidity of so many fellwalkers, largely based on ignorance of the safety rules. David Osselton and a party of boys on the western slopes of Helvellyn met a man who told them that he had in point of fact seen the missing boy in the Keswick 'bus shelter that morning. Further inquiries by the Police found him waiting outside the Ambleside youth hostel to which he had travelled from the hostel in Keswick. The Search Controller had been told the previous evening by the Police that inquiries had been made for this boy in all youth hostels, but without result.

'Our operational headquarters was kept open for a further four hours until all teams were safely off the fell-side. Colin Bolton and Richard Lee did a good job in manning the radio relay station on the cloud-covered summit of Raise throughout the day and the various teams were kept in contact with the Search Controller via their station. They were last off the fell shortly before dark.

'The boy's father, a traveller in clocks, spent some time with us in our search headquarters and a few days later a large-faced electric clock was delivered to the school and now graces the wall of the office which acts as an ops' room during final expeditions and mountain rescue call-outs.

'Later in the Course one of the Mummery Patrol groups of six boys walking to Deepdale was on the roadside near Hartsop corner, below Brotherswater, when they heard a tremendous smash. They ran round the corner and saw a small white car with five occupants which had run into the back of a lorry. Apart from the lorry driver, who was suffering from shock, and the injured occupants there was nobody else present. The group leader, David Hill (Southern Electricity Board), quickly organized his team in a most efficient manner. A middle-aged man and his wife were bleeding badly from cuts to leg and face and the other three occupants were severely shocked. All five were extracted from the car, which was a write-off, and laid on the roadside wrapped in sleeping bags. Wounds were dressed and tea was brewed for the patients while other boys went to a telephone to call for an ambulance, the police and a doctor.

'They then converted the nearby bus shelter into a first aid station for the two more injured people. Whilst waiting for the ambulance they swept the road of glass and wreckage, collected up the patients' scattered belongings and were able to give detailed information to the police and doctor when they arrived. After the patients were taken away the six boys continued their walk to the camp-site.

'Three days later the patients, who had just been discharged from hospital, visited the school to express their thanks to us in person.'

Girls' Courses

As early as 1949 the Outward Bound Trust set up a committee under the chairmanship of Lady David Douglas-Hamilton to consider the merits of applying Outward Bound training to girls. The committee came out in favour of extending the work from boys to girls and the first experimental course was held at the Eskdale Mountain School in 1951. The Central Council for Physical Education seconded one of its staff, Miss Ruth Keeble, to run the first course and, with the help of the Trust's committee, a pattern of training suitable to girls was soon evolved.

At the first courses at Eskdale, climbing, fell-walking and camping were new activities for groups of girls in which three-quarters had never walked farther than the nearest shops and 90 per cent had never done any camping. Yet by the end of the course some groups of four or five were away on a camping expedition of three days and two nights. A group of twelve walked 50 miles in three days, staying at youth hostels for the nights, and another group of twelve canoed in the Esk, carrying their canoes on trek carts for 13 miles of the Pony expedition.

At the first group of courses for girls a wider range of educational activities was organized than had developed in the boys' courses. At different courses these included first aid and home nursing, drama, choral speaking and mime, drawing and painting, puppetry, country dancing and music appreciation. An indoor practical activity that featured in all courses was the construction of canvas and wood canoes.

It was not possible to use the Eskdale Mountain School for more than the occasional girls' course so for the first five years courses were held at one or other of the residential training centres of the Central Council for Physical Recreation. The programme of outdoor activities at these courses varied according to the facilities and equipment of the training centre, but at Bisham Abbey, for example, by the end of the course every student had sailed a dinghy, had ridden a horse on her own and had reached a reasonable competence with a canoe. Each student could also choose to become more than merely acquainted with either sailing, canoeing or riding. The sailors learnt much about the maintenance of dinghies and could handle one unaccompanied. The canoeists could manage rough-water canoeing, overturning, and all had undertaken a three-day canoe expedition. The riders had learnt the rudiments of grooming, feeding and caring for horses and had undertaken several three-hour expeditions in the hills.

As the courses for girls developed they grew richer in content so that some girls were able, if they wished, even to choose farming as a special activity, which meant that they would learn to drive a tractor, to care for stock and to learn some of the skills of fruit or vegetable farming.

The experimental period in the holding of Outward Bound courses for girls ended in 1963, with the establishment of a permanent school for girls at Rhowniar. After twenty years of steady development and adaptation it was to be followed by a period of much more rapid change, for between 1963 and 1970 no fewer than seven new types of course were begun. In these seven years something like a rebirth has taken place in the life of the Outward Bound Schools and the nature of this rebirth must now be described in more detail.

7. NEW COURSES

Seven new types of course have been tried out in the past seven years and most represent not a mere modification of the standard course but a new approach to the needs of adolescents in the critical period between sixteen and nineteen years. Each course has had its enthusiastic promoters but most have had to prove their success to the more conservative and orthodox. Each new course has also had to justify itself during an experimental period and several of the courses have not yet emerged from this phase. Each course represents an attempt to relate the form of adolescent education more closely to modern needs as these have slowly become clearer.

European Courses

The first of these new types of course was perhaps the least radical and was not deliberately planned as an innovation. Nevertheless it can be regarded as related to the likely entry of Great Britain into the Common Market of Europe and to the strengthening of ties with that continent.

The immediate cause of this innovation was the incidence of such a severe epidemic of foot-and-mouth disease in the north-west of England in 1967 that almost all outdoor activities at the two schools of Eskdale and

Ullswater were made impossible. Their staffs were forced to gaze across the boundary fences of their estates and to look in frustration at snow-covered mountains that were now forbidden territory. In this situation the Warden of Ullswater School recalled a series of visits that he and his wife had made to the mountains of the Ardennes, and decided to go on a six-day reconnaissance of the Grand Duchy of Luxembourg. After camping a night in thick snow he drove through wooded gorges to look at a youth hostel which might provide accommodation at Hollenfels. There, at the top of a gorge he found not only the hostel he was looking for, but an ancient castle, unoccupied, and across its drawbridge, a second youth hostel. It was a magnificent site and provided ample accommodation. He drove on to Luxembourg Ville where he put his problem to the Minister responsible for Luxembourg youth work. The Minister and the other officials he met offered to give every assistance to an Outward Bound party at Hollenfels and to give it immediately.

Back in England, the Warden at once seized the opportunity to join in the planning of an overseas course for both Eskdale and Ullswater schools. From this joint European work, there began a strengthening of the bonds between two British Mountain Schools that very naturally had sometimes been tempted into friendly rivalry.

In two weeks, the two Wardens of Eskdale and Ullswater, their deputy wardens, bursars and secretaries had planned two courses to consist of ten days of basic training in the Lake District followed by sixteen days of a modified standard course at Hollenfels. The basic training was made much more of a 'toughening' experience than would be normal because it was realized that conditions in the Luxembourg mountains would be spartan and temperatures would fall much lower than in Westmorland. In spite of foot-and-mouth disease in the Lake District, one expedition was possible—a canoe trip up Ullswater

to a camp-site on wind-swept rocks in sub-zero temperatures. From this camp the patrols canoed to Glen-
ridding and walked over the snow-covered Kirkstone
Pass to Ambleside. An ice-covered quarry was used for
climbing and mountain-rescue work. Back on the school
estate some climbing practice continued, using pitons.
All of this preparation proved to be invaluable in Luxembourg because there the students had to live at times at
temperatures of 32° F. below freezing point

Soon after their arrival in Luxembourg the patrols set
out on a three-day expedition. There was thick snow and
although the route involved no rock-climbing, ice-axes
were needed and used. On the final day of the expedition
the patrols had made such progress that instructors left
each patrol to find its own way back across the forests to
the castle.

After this strenuous expedition there was a 'rest'
period of indoor work, given over largely to environmental
studies. On this type of overseas course, the problem of
integrating intellectual with physical activity is easily
solved since an introduction to the language, the history
and the geography of the country visited is the very
obvious form which it takes. The problem of including
some form of community service in a course is not so
easily solved because the necessary contacts do not exist,
but in Hollenfels students swept the streets of the town
free from the grit, slush, and rubbish always left behind
when heavy snow melts and earned the gratitude of the
villagers.

During the period of indoor activity there were
lectures and discussions led by the assistant editor of
the leading Luxembourg newspaper and the director
of the Chamber of Commerce. In this and in many
informal ways much mutual British–Luxembourg understanding was promoted.

For the second and final expedition of the course the

boys had four days of warm sunshine and blue skies climbing in Luxembourg's beautiful 'little Switzerland' and for this the Outward Bound staff were joined by members of the Luxembourg Alpine Club. The course concluded with a farewell party for roughly equal numbers of Luxembourgers and British at which the main refrain of the Luxembourgers was 'You must come again'.

Mixed Courses

The first experimental course for a mixed group of boys and girls in approximately equal numbers was held at Rhowniar in January 1969. I arrived at Rhowniar on my second visit just as they were beginning to tackle the high ropes. It was at once apparent to me that students and staff were in very good spirits and more than usually enthusiastic. On the ropes some of the girls were a little more frightened than most of the boys but the boys were immensely helpful. All were wearing anoraks and trousers and some of the boys had long hair, so it was often difficult to tell the boys from the girls. I saw one student successfully overcome a difficult part of the circuit and as she swung to the ground I saw a tear of joy running down her face, so I guessed she was a girl. In this activity (and in all the others I saw) it seemed to me that the course was bringing out the best in both boys and girls. The girls seemed more sensible, less 'giggly', and more adult than the girls I had seen earlier on a single-sex course, while the boys were less boisterous, more considerate, and their language noticeably less crude. That this was a fair judgement is borne out by the fact that the school matron found herself with less to do on this mixed course than on courses for girls. Petty ailments, imaginary malaise, and emotional upsets were many fewer. This was partly due to the fact that they were all enjoying themselves so much and partly to an element of pride, neither sex being willing to show weakness in the presence of the other. There had been some fears that a standard course would be too strenuous for the girls but I saw no sign of this. All the girls were in excellent health and spirits and towards the end of the course I thought their 'staying power' was on the whole rather better than that of the boys.

Sometimes, but not often, the boys and girls were engaged in separate activities, as, for example, when the girls were engaged in horse-riding while the boys were at an Army assault course; but in the rock-climbing, in the long 'abseil' down a slate-mine in the dark, in the canoeing and mountain expedition all did the same programme except that on Cader Idris the girls slept in a cottage while the boys slept in tents and the boys carried heavier packs. In the indoor activities such as 'music and move-ment' and drama, the mixture of the sexes was a great source of enrichment. Every instructor told me that the young people in his group worked splendidly together; their attitude to each other was gay, friendly, and natural and in this respect no student had given them a moment's disquiet.

I had an interview with each member of the course on its penultimate day and what they told me reinforced my own very favourable impressions of its success. I did dis-cover two boys who said they had no use for girls and wished they had gone on a boys' rather than a mixed course but all the girls said they would prefer a mixed to a single-sex course.

I had just devised my questionnaire for use with the students of the Devon School, so I was able to use the same questions verbally with this mixed group of boys and girls. When I compared their replies later with the written replies from Devon students a number of not unexpected contrasts appeared. On both courses the highest ratings for quality were given to the teaching of the school staff but the members of the mixed course were much more enthusiastic about the equipment of the school. Only 10 per cent of students on the men's course gave a high rating to the quality of the daily religious service but on the mixed course no less than 70 per cent gave it a high rating. The same difference showed itself in the high rating given to the educational and cultural activities of the mixed course (by 65 per cent of the students) compared with the low proportion of 10 per cent on a single-sex course. In the men's course the highest ratings of all were given to the increased physical fitness and general euphoria experienced by the end of the course. In the mixed course the highest rating was given to the experience of team-work and the value of living with a small group of individuals from contrasting backgrounds. Much higher ratings were given by the members of the mixed course to its general educational and cultural activities, and to an appreciation of the beauty of the countryside.

In providing a number of mixed courses the Outward Bound Trust is following a general trend in higher education. The year 1970 has seen the admission of mixed groups for the first time to Oxford and Cambridge colleges, which have been divided into male and female ever since women have entered the universities there.

Extension Courses

A high proportion of the students with whom I talked on my visits to the Schools have told me that they would greatly like to come back to a second course after the interval of a year or two. It is not surprising, therefore, that some wardens began to think of the kind of course that might be arranged for ex-students, who would need something on the lines of a senior course but more challenging. The warden of Rhowniar, therefore, planned an experimental course for an almost equal number of instructors and past students which took the form of a long expedition from Wales to the island of Skye in Scotland. At the centre of the idea was the project to bring an Outward Bound Group to Skye to join with local people in turning an old disused one-teacher school at Torrin on the shores of Loch Elapin into an Alpine-style adventure centre for the youth of Skye. It was planned to take a local group on a canoe expedition, to give them not only a taste of a new activity but to train them at the same time. The weather began fine so a start was made on the canoeing. The Outward Bound students first refreshed their own skills or learnt them for the first time and then took over and taught the youth-club pupils. When the weather deteriorated work was done on the Torrin hut and when the sun came out Eagles Crag was climbed and the eyrie of a golden eagle visited. In the second week of the course the weather changed and snow began to fall on the hills, but a party of walkers and a party of climbers explored the north of the island. In spite of the snow there was good climbing in the Red Hills and the Cullins Mountains. The party completed their work on the Torrin centre, making use of prefabricated material prepared by the Inverness Technical College, fitting the old school up with bunks and repainting walls and doors before leaving for their journey to the South.

In Chapter 9, all the evidence quoted shows that the influence of a single Outward Bound Course, even though it is so short, has a lasting effect on some 80 per cent of those who experience it. Nevertheless, it is short, and at its present period of twenty-six days is shorter than it was originally. The effects of a course might be much more lasting, one would imagine, if a single course were followed by a refresher course held not less than a year and not more than three years afterwards. The arguments in favour of developing this type of course are strengthened by the fact that strong reasons have been advanced for shortening the standard course even more. The first reason is financial: sponsors find it increasingly difficult to find the students' fees and some 30 per cent of them want to see a shorter and cheaper course provided. The second, and much the more important, reason is that as more and more industrial apprentices attend week-night courses of further education or day-release classes, both they and their employers are reluctant to see them miss three whole weeks of classes. If these forces produce some shortening of the standard course it will become even more important for the schools to organize regular refresher or extension courses. In the large group survey already described 87 per cent of students stated that they would accept an invitation to attend such a course and 39 per cent of sponsors expressed their willingness to find the fees.

The Eskdale and Moray Schools both undertook early experiments in the holding of extension courses and the experimental period can now be said to be over. Such a course is now generally for about half the number of students on a standard course or less, i.e. for 50 or less students and for a period of not longer than two weeks. The first week of the course is spent in the school and is devoted to the revision of previously learnt skills such as climbing or canoeing, to a toughening up period of physical education, to the discussion of topics of national and international importance, and to an ecological study of the region to be explored in the following week.

The second week of the course starts with a long over-land trek to a little explored region where ecological studies are combined with more difficult climbing or more adventurous canoeing or more hazardous sailing than was appropriate for an inexperienced group. The course concludes with a short review period back at the school.

Different methods of recruitment for the extension

courses were used at the two schools first experimenting in this field. At Eskdale, the warden wrote to a group of past students whom he thought would like to attend, or who would benefit more than others from a further course. The cost would then fall on the students themselves, except for the few who could persuade their employers to meet it. This financial deterrent resulted in the recruitment of a self-selected group of extremely keen students. For quite different reasons, the group of forty-eight past students of the Moray School who attended its first extension course in the autumn of 1968 were also a highly selected group of very keen students. The warden had looked through his past lists of 2,000 students and selected 200 whom he considered to possess the qualities that would ensure the success of an experimental course. He had then written to their employers and asked them to find the fees of £30 a head which the course would cost. The 20 per cent of employers who had found the fees for a second course must have considered their employees to be of high quality. I was myself able to attend the first week of the course at Moray and found immediately that the Moray method of recruitment had gathered together a most intelligent, able, and almost over-enthusiastic group of men between the ages of 20 and forty, who were preparing eagerly to enjoy a projected expedition to the Cape Wrath region of the northern Highlands.

My visit to the extension course at Moray took place at an early stage of my survey of the work of the schools and I was particularly anxious to provoke past students into a critical or even adverse review of their experiences at an initial standard course. In this I completely failed. They had nothing but praise for every aspect of their first courses. Assessments of different aspects of the standard course for both quality of provision and personal importance, which later gave percentages as low as 10 per cent or between 10 and 20 per cent, simply produced

100 per cent from this group. The only effect my critical questions produced was to turn the subjects of my inquiry into propagandists for Outward Bound ideas.

In the preliminary week of basic training at the Moray School two aspects of the work struck me with great force and convinced me that ideally every student who attended an initial standard course should follow this up with an extension course. The first was the very high standard of the political, religious, and sociological discussions organized by the warden. The greater maturity of the students and their eager desire to discover each other's viewpoint made these discussion periods lively and, I felt certain, of great value to the participants.

The second aspect of the preliminary part of the extension course that impressed itself forcibly on my mind was the extremely original and successful sessions of physical education which the warden had invented to bring a group of physically flabby men in the short period of a week up to such a high pitch of physical fitness that they were all ready to undertake an arduous walking and climbing expedition in difficult mountainous country.

During the camping period of the Moray extension course at Cape Wrath, particular thought was given to the organization of sessions of community service, which, in extension courses, can be given an emphasis inappropriate for younger groups. This took the form of a farming project to help a group of local crofters who, without aid, would not have been able to complete the winter digging of drainage ditches on a pasture reclamation scheme.

At the second extension course organized at Moray in February 1970, the group was rather larger and included also a large group of senior men from industry and educational administration. In the basic training week at the school, the physical education sessions included a substantial section of work given over to judo training by the Scottish National coach, Andrew Bull. The second half of the course was spent at Morvich on Loch Duich, which had been acquired as an annexe to the Moray School, and there a programme of ice and snow training activities was planned. In the event there was no lack of snow and much of the training was done in conditions of impending blizzard. The bad weather made training difficult and when it made them impossible a scheme of help to local farmers badly hit by the blizzard took their place. In addition, four members of the course staff joined a police mountain-rescue team that went to the help of a party of climbers from St. Andrews University who were injured on a peak and had been overtaken by the blizzard. Two climbers were brought down, one with an injured ankle and the other with a fractured skull.

Rover Courses

Unlike most of the American Outward Bound Schools, the work of the British Schools, and their particular kind of success, is due to the fact that each school has buildings in which good and appropriate equipment, workshops, laboratories, libraries, classrooms, and common rooms can allow a series of short courses to be run efficiently. Moreover, at each school there is a substantial residential staff, with wives, children, and friends, who give that firm family feeling to the courses, which has already been described. The sort of experience provided for past students on extension courses by the wardens of Eskdale, Rhowniar, and Moray depended much less upon this central provision of a school and much more upon the development of a simpler hutted camp-site at some distance from the school. Following on the experience of 'Rover' courses with past students the wardens of most schools have also experimented with the establishment of school 'annexes' and the planning of Rover courses for students aged sixteen to nineteen. As with the extension courses, Rover courses have generally been organized for only small parties of twenty or so students. With such a small group there are special advantages and some disadvantages. Students and instructors live, sleep, and eat in close proximity. This makes living together a more demanding affair but it can press rather heavily on the staff members of the group. On the other hand, with such a course the staff can consist mainly of young instructors seconded from institutions of higher education, from the police or from junior training posts in industry, and so they may be only two or three years older than the students. The whole course can be planned in a more flexible and informal manner than a standard course and this makes it possible to adapt more easily to the rapidly changing weather conditions of the British Isles. On such a course, self-discipline becomes a more important point of character growth than self-confidence. Community service is rather easier to organize, especially when the camp is sited in a National Park, but on the other hand carefully graded training sessions are much less easy to administer and have to give way to 'learning on the job'. With such a balance of advantages and disadvantages the future of Rover courses is still a little uncertain, but their popularity at Outward Bound Schools in the United States may indicate the growth of a similar popularity here, particularly in the summer.

Special Group Courses

When they organize their own courses, the British Schools deliberately recruit students with as widely different backgrounds as possible. Nevertheless, it was almost inevitable that sooner or later organizations or homogeneous groups should ask the wardens of schools to organize Outward Bound courses for their own groups. The inevitable has happened and courses have been organized for students from colleges of education, colleges of technology, for the police, for a group of headmasters and, most unusual of all, for the members and coaches of the British Olympic hockey team.

Special group courses such as these take as their starting point the essential characteristics of the standard course but the special characteristics of a group are used to give some special relevance to each of the aspects in turn. Thus, for example, trainee bricklayers naturally find an avenue for community service in the building of children's playground equipment, headmasters can be attached to the patrols or watches of a standard course as educational 'advisers', and professional athletes can discover that 'training' is not just a matter of the body but even more of the mind. It was in a special course for the England Olympic hockey team that the warden of the Moray School was able to use the unconventional methods of training which, over the years, he had invented to bring even the physically handicapped to the utmost of their bodily potential, and which, even with highly skilled athletes, he found to produce better and more lasting effects than more orthodox methods.

Sponsors Courses

One special group course that may influence very greatly the way in which standard courses are followed up in students' places of employment is a type of course arranged specially for older men and women who have sponsored students to courses or who as training or youth officers or teachers in higher education have been concerned with their selection. Such courses include executives or even parents. The main aim of these courses is to help those who may be in a position to follow up the work of an Outward Bound course with students when they return to their employment or place of education. Sponsors courses last about a week and are planned to take place side by side with a standard course so that the older m em   f the course can both sample its activities and see its influence on the students. No pressure is brought to bear on members to take part in any activity they feel is too much for them, but most are so attracted by the activities that they tend to overdo things and often confess to a secret desire to jump into their cars and go home after a day or two—but the chief instructor who acts as their group-instructor brings them over this 'hump' and sees that they do less, mix with the students more, learn their reactions, appreciate the insistence on safety rules, and generally absorb the spirit of the course. The presence of a group of senior men from a wide variety of occupations acts as a tonic to the staff and is good for the school.

At a recent sponsors course at the Moray School one of its members designed the following questionnaire which, with the warden's permission, he sent out to members of the course as soon as they had returned to their homes:

1. Have you enjoyed the Course? If yes, why? If not, why not?
2. What do you think the Course has done for you as an individual?
3. Do you think there is room for improvement at the School?
4. What is your opinion of the Physical Education at the School?
5. What do you see as the advantages of an Outward Bound course?
6. Has the experience of a Sponsors Course influenced you as regards sending students to a School?
7. Do you consider a Sponsors Course should be of a month's duration?

8. Would you be prepared to take part in a month's course?

The warden of Moray kindly sent me the replies to this questionnaire, which may be summarized in the following form:

1. All, without exception, had enjoyed the course, giving as their main reason that it had achieved its purpose in giving them an insight into the nature of Outward Bound work.

2. The replies to the question about the value of the course to each individual bore a surprising resemblance to the replies of ordinary students, selecting for praise physical euphoria, the enjoyment of learning a new skill, or the appreciation of companionship in an atmosphere of simplicity and rest.

3. From this group of older men there came many suggestions for improvement in such things as the provision of better common rooms, the addition of a projects room, or the greater use of the mass-media of communication.

4. The praise of the physical education was universal.

5. The advantages of a standard course were given in identically the same form as in the replies to the large questionnaire study described in Chapter 5.

6. 85 per cent of members said that they would in future work to send more students to Outward Bound courses.

7 and 8. There was almost universal agreement that a week's course was sufficient, although one or two thought it might be a few days longer.

One of the training officers who attended a sponsors course at the Devon School wrote afterwards to the warden as follows:

'Before attending this Course I had had no direct involvement or communication with Outward Bound. As a layman, therefore, my image of the organization had been the "hearty physical" one which would equip (or assist the student to equip himself) with a possibly more balanced outlook on life because of bodily fitness and well-being.

'By my own observation and as a result of the answers I have received from students and officers of the organization, I have now become aware of a kind of spiritual rejuvenation which results from participation in the Course for, at least, many people. I believe it is very difficult for the "outsider" to perceive how far-reaching and fundamental are the intellectual processes involved, but some of these at least became apparent to me.'

Welfare Courses

The rescue work and community service elements in all standard courses have already been described. Increasingly, the schools have found places on standard courses for those who are physically handicapped or who have suffered in one way or another from faults in their upbringing. Students sponsored by the Home Office fall into this category. The number of such students accepted for a single standard course, although small, has been growing over the years. In a recent course at the Ullswater School it was discovered that a blind student working closely with a paired sighted student could take a full part in the normal activities of the course. In September 1969 a small experimental course was planned at the Moray School for a group of fifteen boys 'on probation' and the five probation officers responsible for their care, which showed the Outward Bound commitment to the field of welfare courses as never before.

Some extracts from the report of the director of the course at Moray indicates the nature of the lessons learnt from the first tentative venture in this field. He wrote at the conclusion of the seven-day course an assessment both of its rationale and its limitations in the following terms:

'In both Approved School and Borstal entries there is often a pattern of delinquency or serious conflict within the family group. Both these factors contribute strongly in bringing the boy into conflict with authority and "normal" society. The boy has often suffered, through neglect by parents, or, possibly, through the loss of one, or both of them. Misunderstanding, insecurity, inadequate schooling or (and this is a trend I see as increasing), he has been put into "care" at an early age and has become strongly institutionalised.

'If any real changes are to be brought about in the attitude of these young lads it is vital that their environment be changed.

'This then is point one in the reason for my wishing to experiment by having these groups in an Outward Bound setting. My second lies in the problems confronting probation officers who are charged with caring for or guiding those who have been discharged from a delinquent institution or those who have been given a probation order in the hope that commitment to an institution can be avoided. . . . I have felt for a long time that it would be useful to get the officers and their charges together, in our type of environment, for a period. I felt that by working together a greater rapport could be developed and that the officer would gain, in the more informal and relaxed Outward Bound situation, a deeper understanding of a lad's personality traits and problems.

'Most instructors were amazed at how suddenly a boy's mood could change and this unpredictable conduct made it almost impossible to treat any two boys alike. All boys seemed determined to retain their individuality and few were anxious to form any loyalties with their own small group of their own Watch. On the other hand practically all of the boys soon identified themselves with the School and referred to equipment and School as "ours".

'During a group discussion in the dormitory, all boys expressed an extremely high regard for staff members and they were all amazed how never at any time during the course had any of the staff lost his temper. This amount of self-control and tolerance was completely foreign to nearly all the boys but the mere fact that it was noticed, indicated how they could perhaps be influenced by example.

'The Probation Officers and the Borstal Officer were certain that during this week they had been able to establish a much better and deeper relationship with the boys they had brought on the course. It was doubtful if such a relationship could be established under normal circumstances, irrespective of how long interview sessions lasted. The shared experiences during activities, sharing the same dormitory and being able to observe each other at close quarters had opened new doors to a much deeper and more intimate relationship that would prove an ideal base from which to help the Probationer tackle his particular problem. The Probationers also shared in this experience and they now had much more confidence in their Supervising Officers and were much more able to communicate with them.

'From the present group it was thought that 65 per cent could quite easily be invited to join another course; 25 per cent were unsuitable because of lack of intellect or physique; and the remainder were totally unsuitable because of their disturbed emotional state.

'While it is not suggested that Outward Bound should be considered as an alternative to Approved Schools or Borstals it would be interesting to compare the cost involved in keeping a boy at each of these Institutions, assuming that success in halting some of the boy's previous anti-social tendencies was rapid.'

The comments of a probation officer on the course were put in the following words:

'My job has been made much easier in relation to the

three boys who completed the course with me. Already I have gained more knowledge and more insight into their problems and we now have a much deeper mutual trust in each other. I also consider that there are a great many boys who would benefit from courses of this nature; boys who are on the fringe of trouble and who inevitably become involved either through boredom, for kicks, or simply out of not knowing anything better to do. I firmly believe that a great many of the so-called "delinquents" would respond to the challenge of Outward Bound and having done so, they could not help but assist in their own character development which in turn would make them more useful members of Society.'

A second course of the same kind was held in April 1970. The group of boys involved was still kept very small but the scope of recruitment was widened. The students included some from Approved Schools, some from Borstals, and some who were the subjects of a probation order.

Lessons learnt in the earlier course made it possible to experiment in some new directions—in, for example, holding sessions which, though they were not called so, were group-therapy sessions.

Rock-climbing and swimming again proved extremely popular with the boys and two did exceptionally well in these. One had a new climb on the quarry face named after him and he also gained the Bronze Medallion in Life Saving. Another passed both the Bronze Medallion Award and the Award of Merit in Life Saving. Neither had training in this prior to the course. Eight awards were gained in all and three non-swimmers were taught to swim. All the boys had identified with the school by mid-week, virtually no time was wasted, and each of the boys gained confidence in himself, some much more than others, but all expressed positive feelings on some aspect of training.

The course concluded with a 'post mortem' conference attended by the staff of the course and officers, social workers and educationalists concerned with work for juvenile delinquents. It was agreed that the success of the second course was partly due to the fact that the young men coming on the course had been fully prepared and briefed by their own social workers (probation officers) and because the social workers themselves had been brought together before the course began for an induction course.

The work of this conference was divided into three parts. Part one was a detailed analysis of every boy's performance in relation to his previous behaviour patterns. The second part was a comparison of the second course with the earlier course (at which everyone present had taken part). The third part was a discussion between social workers, directors of social work and school staff on the best means by which a follow-up to the course might be made.

With the conclusion of a third course at the end of 1970 the experimental period may be regarded as over. All that is needed now is the finance to support future courses, for they are more expensive to run than any others.

In Scotland, where a growing group of social workers has become interested in this new development of remedial care, such financial help may be forthcoming, but in England and Wales this line of development still has to make its way, though the outlook is propitious because the probation service is to be expanded and training facilities remodelled. Certain types of offenders who have previously been sent to prison may, in the future, do a period of community service work under the joint control of the probation service and the voluntary agencies. In such a scheme, offenders could make some repayment to the community for damage they have inflicted. In addition there would not be the difficult problem of adjustment to civil life for the prisoner who intends to go straight at the end of his sentence. Before embarking on this new type of penal care, the officers of the probation service and the voluntary agencies who are likely to be involved will clearly benefit greatly from a preliminary training as members of an Outward Bound welfare course.

8.   CITY CHALLENGE

The most radical departure from accustomed routine in
the organization of Outward Bound courses was the
result of the desire of Captain Fuller, the most experienced of the wardens, to devise a course that might con-
front young people with social problems to which they
might never otherwise be exposed. He envisaged a three
weeks' course that would bring into a large industrial city
a group of young men, recruited from widely varied backgrounds, who would provide several different kinds of
community service to the civic authorities. The operation
was thought of as the joint enterprise of a group of
Outward Bound instructors and of the local officers of the
youth, education or welfare services of the chosen city,
and was called 'City Challenge'.

Captain Fuller did not have to look far to find his first
city for an experimental course. In Yorkshire, the first
warden of Aberdovey, now a member of the management
committee, was deputy education officer and in Leeds,
the director, John Taylor, was sympathetic to the idea of
the experiment and prepared to give strong local co-
operation. So Leeds was chosen for the first 1967 City
Challenge Course and Jim Hogan acted as chairman of
an organizing committee. Captain Fuller himself came as
course director, with the assistant youth officer for Leeds
as his deputy director. The staff were drawn from Out-

ward Bound, Leeds and officers of the West Riding Authority. It was because of this that the West Riding was able to provide an important nucleus of experimental staff for all subsequent courses. Thirty-seven students enrolled for the course so that the ratio of staff to students was high, but this was very necessary in a new course where the snags and problems were unknown.

The community service work undertaken was of several kinds, in each of which continuity was maintained by the work of small groups of three or four students, each one of which did its stint of duty and was then replaced by another.

One set of groups worked in the evenings either at the Salvation Army Hostel or the St. George's Crypt where beds and a little free food were available for the old, decrepit, lonely wanderers who had no homes to go to at night, were in a mental state which had removed all desire to work, and were in the lowest stages of destitution. The work to be done consisted in doling out clothing, soup, and bread to men whose only possessions were ragged parcels of extra clothing.

Another set of groups served as porters at the main city hospitals from 7 p.m. to 1 a.m., when extra manual help was gladly welcomed. This experience brought home to them the severity of some social problems, for many of the admissions were the result of assaults, rape, drunkenness, and child neglect. It was some of the terrible injuries inflicted on young children that brought home to students the pitifulness of the human condition.

Another set of groups offered their services to the headmaster of a school with a 70 per cent coloured immigrant population, where he used them in the supervision of extra-classroom activities.

A small group reported daily to the City of Leeds Welfare Centre so that they could go out and give help in the homes of physically handicapped people and those so old that their homes had become neglected or insanitary. This work took students into the very worst slum areas and brought them most quickly and starkly into contact with human tragedy. A different kind of contact with the old and helpless came from visits to the geriatric wards of a hospital.

Another set of groups attended daily for a period of training with the city fire brigade.

Every member of the course at some time did a spell of practical work in the building of a children's adventure playground under the guidance of the City Parks director. Before the course had ended the work was complete, and it was full of active noisy children.

In addition to the main programme of social service, there was a personal programme of physical education at the Carnegie College of Physical Education, where the students lived. The main purposes of these daily periods of judo, rock-climbing, swimming or canoeing were to give members of the course a time of physical recreation away from the emotionally demanding social services of the course and to strengthen the team spirit of the working groups in more relaxed situations than those of personal service to others.

At the conclusion of the course the Director of Education for Leeds assessed its value as follows:

'Nobody who heard the groups discussing their experiences could fail to realize the psychological shock they received, or to be impressed by the responsibility and resilience with which they reacted. All who have considerable dealings with young people are aware of the deep reservoir of willingness to serve which flows into the youth voluntary services in the developing countries and our industrial cities. "City Challenge" threw an interesting new light on the use which can be made of the goodwill and energy which is there. . . . This experience convinced the people concerned in Leeds that there is a place for controlled and guided voluntary effort within the statutory and professional structure of the social services.'

The main purpose of the first pilot experiment at Leeds was to gain experience. The director and staff were quick to learn the lessons of the pilot course and to propose that a second should be mounted at Leeds in 1968. As always happens with pilot experiments it was realized that a course as demanding as City Challenge called for a much more thorough preparation of both students and staff than they had been given before the first course opened. This was particularly necessary for the staff, which was not an expert team, long prepared for this particular work, but the choice available at the time from the youth service, the education authorities of Leeds and the Outward Bound Trust. There was discussion also of ways in which activities begun on the course might be continued by local groups and organizations such as the Outward Bound Association, students of the Duke of Edinburgh Award Scheme, the scouts and youth club members. So far as recruitment for the course was concerned, it was recommended that this should be more selective, with a majority of older adolescents, but including also a few young immigrants, both white and coloured. There were also many practical suggestions made for the improvement of course organization.

The lessons learnt in the first City Challenge course were made use of in a second course held in Leeds in the spring of 1968. This time the training team had a preparatory week together in Leeds before the course began. The group organization of the course was also strengthened. The forty students of the course were divided into six syndicates, named after six districts of the city, each syndicate under the guidance of a tutor and living in rooms next to each other. The general programme followed similar lines to the 1967 programme except that the practical project of building an adventure playground, which had proved over-ambitious, was replaced by a scheme for transforming the Bear Pit, built in 1840, into a garden for old people.

In the second course at Leeds, the average age of the groups was eighteen plus, and twelve students were over the age of twenty. These much more mature groups not only did better work than the first but gained much more from the experience. The reports received from the various centres of service showed how much had been learnt from the experimental course.

In the wards of Meanwood Hospital for the mentally sub-normal where there is a grave shortage of nursing staff and 60 per cent are coloured, the students were soon established as auxiliaries to the nurses. One of the patients said, 'They do us all good. They have brought new life and laughter to the wards'. In the end, it became almost a pathetically one-sided relationship with patients eagerly waiting for and accepting every word, smile, and action directed at them by the students.

Students who acted as porters at the casualty reception centres of the two large city hospitals had experiences of a varying intensity, but in the second course they were able to give more thought to the care of the families of the casualties and to find ways of helping them.

At St. George's Crypt, the work led on more easily to a discussion of the social problems of the transients and unemployed because the seminar which followed was directed by the warden of the Crypt.

A housing 'task force' sometimes ran into surprising situations. A mother, deserted by her husband, was found trying to cope with three legitimate and six illegitimate children. An elderly spinster, confined to a wheelchair for fifty years, was discovered living in a room darkened by the growth of a high hedge; she had been unable to find any neighbour willing or able to cut the hedge, to let in the light and to enable her to watch the ebb and flow of life in the street.

These, and other experiences were often strong meat for the younger students, and there was great need for special care by tutors, and for staff meetings at which students' progress was carefully but unobtrusively watched.

At the end of the course its lessons were carefully noted. It was realized that more thought was needed in planning continued help once the students had finished their period of service. It was suggested that there should be a careful selection of students for courses of this kind, but this would only be possible if it were combined with considerable earlier publicity and pre-arrangement. It was also suggested that the value of a City Challenge Course might be enhanced if the team was composed of equal numbers of men and women, such equality extending also to each syndicate. The possibility of improving the pre-liminary staff training was also explored. The fact that the joint staff had experienced a preliminary week-end at an Outward Bound School and then a week of planning together in Leeds had done much to weld them into a united force. One suggestion was that, in the preliminary week at Leeds, staff members might give some time to working themselves at the various centres of service, and should meet continually as a seminar group under the guidance of a staff tutor. Perhaps the most important proposal made at the conclusion of the course was that the period of student participation in each activity should be longer and continuous.

These proposals of a joint Outward Bound and local authority conference at Leeds were translated into practice on further courses held in the cities of Cardiff, Manchester, and Edinburgh. After the first two courses held at Leeds it was impossible for Captain Fuller to continue to organize and direct these new activities as well as to meet the commitments of a full-time Warden of the Sea School at Aberdovey. The only sensible alternative was to select someone who had served on the staff of all the previous courses. Mr. David Gibson was the obvious choice. He was a Youth Officer on the staff of the West Riding Education Authority and they agreed to second him for approximately half of his time each year to plan and direct the three City Challenge courses per annum that it was anticipated would be organized. By 1970, a firm pattern of operation emerged for City Challenge courses in large cities. In the meantime, Jim Hogan, who had made these developments a matter for his constant concern, support, and guidance, came to the conclusion that an experiment should be tried with a course not in a large city, but in a small industrial town. With his encouragement, a City Challenge course was run most successfully at the small Yorkshire industrial town of Batley, and then, using the lessons learnt there, at a town of about the same size— also in Yorkshire—Pontefract. It may be useful to conclude this account of the growth of the City Challenge courses by giving some details of this fifth City Challenge course, held in the Spring of 1970.

The account of this course at Pontefract, in contrast to the early experiments at Leeds, shows how far and how fast educational thinking had moved in three years. It shows also that creative thinking can often emerge from the joint work of two bodies of teachers drawn from two very different types of educational activity—in this case from work with a voluntary agency and work with the statutory youth service.

The students at Pontefract had been recruited with the care recommended at the conclusion of earlier courses. Seventeen were men, averaging 18·8 years in age, and sixteen were girls, averaging 19·3 years. Four students were between the ages of twenty-three and twenty-five and two of these were married. The students came from all parts of England and Scotland, and were from very varied working and social backgrounds.

The course was directed by Captain Fuller's successor as the organizer of the City Challenge courses, David Gibson, who has already been mentioned. Of the eight group tutors who made up the staff, two were Outward Bound instructors (a woman from Rhowniar and a man from Devon), three were West Riding youth leaders, and three were teachers with special responsibilities in their schools for youth work.

The week of preliminary staff briefing was held at the Bramley Grange College of the West Riding Authority. During this week the aims and administration of the course were discussed as in earlier courses, but, on two days, staff members worked at a psychiatric hospital and a geriatric hospital, and on a third day each group tutor worked at the centre of service which was to be his special responsibility.

The course began with a period of briefing for the students, chiefly through group seminars. In addition, there were talks by a children's officer, a senior nursing officer of the psychiatric hospital, and the director of the Salvation Army Hostel. There was also a visit to a modern colliery in the neighbourhood.

In the social service activities of the course, the principle followed was to organize two or three days of continuous work by a single group at a particular centre. For each student this worked out as three consecutive days at a psychiatric hospital, three days as a home help under the guidance of the children's department and probation service, two days at a Salvation Army hostel, two days at a geriatric hospital, two days at the Sue Ryder Home for sick and disabled foreigners, and two days with a pre-school playgroup.

As in earlier courses, community projects were undertaken—half the group rebuilding a youth club, and the

other half renovating a school playground. In this way the
balance of the course was held, with fourteen days of
demanding social work and seminar discussion, four days
of briefing and de-briefing, and three free days when each
student could choose to go on a climbing or walking
expedition, write letters or just be idle. The seminars
held a central place in the course. On each evening before
a group worked at a particular centre of service, the
appropriate tutor held a briefing seminar. The running
seminars rarely finished their discussions under $1\frac{1}{2}$ hours,
and 2 hours was the usual period demanded by the
students. The staff of the course spent even longer on
them. The usual Outward Bound practice of a mid-
course discussion of students' progress lasted for two
afternoons, and the final staff meeting for five hours.
These simple facts of timing are mentioned only to
indicate that on a City Challenge course different staff-
student relationships develop from those which have
already been described and observed on standard courses.
They may have the same or a similar balance of advantages
and disadvantages that were found to develop on 'Rover'
courses in England and mobile courses in America,
because they spring from the fact that an instructor and
his group are sharing very close quarters in an identical
experience. On a standard course, questions of student
discipline rarely arise because the skill of the instructor
and the hazards of an experience impose a natural discipline which soon comes to be accepted without any
feeling of restraint. On a City Challenge course, discipline
is not a problem for the very different reason that in the
face of the desperate needs and problems of others,
peccadilloes of personal behaviour are seen to be the trivia
that they are in reality. Although instructors and the
members of their groups vary in maturity and social experience, they face a developing situation together and
the very openness of the situation and the complex human

problems it reveals bring instructors and students very close to each other in their attempts to interpret what they have jointly experienced. It is in this respect that a City Challenge course differs from any other form of voluntary social service. The willingness of young people to serve the needs of others is harnessed on such a course, but its prime purpose is to promote their own growth to maturity by giving them an insight into some of the very serious social problems of our time.

The steady growth of City Challenge courses would have imposed an intolerable burden on the officers of the Outward Bound Trust had it not been for the fact that the Education Authority of the West Riding, after the initial secondment of David Gibson, later agreed to his immediate release from their service. This appointment made it possible for the Trust to accept an invitation from the government of Northern Ireland early in 1970 to send a small team to visit Belfast and Londonderry, cities torn by political and religious dissension, and to discuss with some twenty youth organizations there the degree to which local City Challenge courses might contribute to their well-being and improve community relations. This visit led to the holding of a course for a mixed group of Catholic and Protestant men and women in Londonderry in the late autumn of 1970. It was directed by David Gibson and he found it, if anything, even more rewarding than earlier courses which he had directed in the West Riding. He and some others are now considering how best to follow up a City Challenge course in a situation that makes all social problems more difficult because of the deeply rooted prejudices and the quick resort to violence of individuals and organized groups.

THE INFLUENCE OF
OUTWARD BOUND

When my first round of visits to Outward Bound Schools
was finished and I had talked to some 500 students I was
obliged to accept their nearly unanimous view that attendance at a course would influence them for many years. I
received this impression at first with incredulity, but was
obliged to pay attention to it because the same view was
expressed, only more strongly, by past students taking
part in extension courses. So I began to think of ways of
testing this general view of the lasting influence of Outward Bound courses and at the same time studying in
more detail the precise nature of their influence. Such
a study is not easy to make.

Outward Bound courses are short and their influence
cannot be easily disentangled from the successive impacts
of influences coming from a student's work, home, friends,
and many others. The ideal method to use in exploring a
situation of this kind is to repeat any follow-up study of
a group of Outward Bound students with a carefully
matched control group, exposed, if possible, to exactly
the same or very similar environmental forces as the group
under study. The control group method can be used
with success when the group studied is fairly homogeneous and its members live during the follow-up period
in an identical or very similar environment. Thus the
follow-up study of the influence of courses of training for
teachers who proceed to work in primary schools is one

in which a control group method can prove useful. But
the basis on which students are recruited for Outward
Bound courses deliberately produces a student group with
the widest possible differences of background. In fact,
students come from schools, the armed forces, the police,
the fire service, heavy industry, banking, Approved
Schools, and so on. In addition, between the ages of
sixteen and nineteen young people are rapidly changing
their environment—from school to university or apprenticeship and from home to lodgings, and are very
difficult to track down.

If these difficulties are overcome, a further difficulty
presents itself. When should the follow-up study be
carried out? If the influence of the course is strong, it will
last over a period of years, yet the further we get away
from it, the less reliable will be the memory of ex-students
and, if a postal method of follow-up is used, the smaller
will be the percentage of replies received to letters or
questionnaires. And this percentage cannot be allowed to
fall too low or else a sample study, however randomly
selected, may not be typical of the larger group the sample
is intended to represent.

It was clear that some of these questions could only be
answered after one or two pilot follow-up studies had
been made with small groups of students, and that a
control group method of study would have to be ruled
out. The best that seemed possible was to carry out a
number of different follow-up studies and to give serious
consideration only to those conclusions or figures where
they were identical or in close agreement even though
obtained in quite different ways. In particular, it would
be important to look at agreements or disagreements that
might occur between the views of students and of their
sponsors, employers, or parents. With this in mind a
study was carried out with the past students of a single
school and then a large-scale study of a group of 3,000

students who had experienced an Outward Bound course not less than six months nor more than eighteen months before their views were canvassed.

One of the surprising results of this inquiry was to show that the firm belief of sponsors and students alike is that the influence of a single Outward Bound course is very persistent: 55 per cent of sponsors believe that it lasts for life, 38 per cent that it lasts for several years, and only 7 per cent that the influence is short-lived. The percentages for students are even higher than this, being 67, 28, and 5 per cent respectively. The students' estimates of the period of influence does not vary much between the best and the worst students, though the worst are much more critical of their courses than the best; and there is also no significant difference between the figures for students from different educational or working backgrounds or of different ages and histories.

A special study made at the Moray School turned out to be of particular value. It was an inquiry made of students who had attended courses at the school in each of the years from 1964 to 1968. Such an inquiry makes students' estimates of the influence of a course less a matter of guesswork and much more a matter of experience. If we compare the views of students who have just finished a course, and so are guessing what its influence may be, with those of students who look back over a period of five years, we have the figures for an estimate of the duration of influence.

For students in 1968/9 courses (%)	*For students in 1964/5 courses* (%)
72 influence for life	64 influence for life
23 influence for several years	32 influence for several years
5 influence for a few months	4 influence for a few months

The analysis of the results of this large-scale survey showed that sponsors and students alike were in very close agreement that the courses produced character development of a kind that can be mainly grouped under the headings of (i) increased self-confidence, (ii) greater maturity, and (iii) greater awareness of the needs of others and greater ability to mix well. For example:

(i) 86 per cent of students believed they had increased in self-confidence during the course and 70 per cent of sponsors reported observing a marked change in them.

(ii) 78 per cent of students believed they had increased in general maturity and 73 per cent of sponsors agreed.

(iii) 64 per cent of students believed they had become more aware of the needs of others or improved in their ability to mix well, whilst 43 per cent of sponsors reported noticing this change.

Again, the analysis by students of the ways in which they had benefited by an Outward Bound course was more optimistic than that of sponsors but not greatly so, and the agreement of view is surprisingly high.

As a more obvious test of the value of a course, sponsors reported that 19 per cent of students had received promotion as a result of attending courses, and the students' figure was slightly higher at 22 per cent. The more optimistic students' figure may be due to a difference in degree between sponsors and students; the former may well believe that in some cases promotion has been due to their own training courses rather than to an Outward Bound course. The true figure may perhaps be that 20 per cent of students are helped to secure promotion at work as a result of attending an Outward Bound course.

The survey also asked students to what extent they had continued to practise one or more of the outdoor skills learnt at a course or had been encouraged by their course to undertake some form of voluntary or statutory youth service work or to continue in some form the rescue or community service activities encountered.

Between 60 and 70 per cent of students reported that after finishing an Outward Bound course they had continued to practise one or more of the outdoor skills learnt, particularly walking and canoeing, and the same high proportion spoke of the enrichment of leisure time activities that had resulted. About 30 per cent reported that they had found their way into voluntary or statutory youth work, which must be very encouraging to the devoted workers in this field, who often gravely lack part-time leaders. The percentage of students who subsequently found their way into rescue or community service work varied from 14 to 42 per cent in different inquiries and on the average this figure is lower than for the entry into youth service work. This is perhaps not surprising since community service work that is sustained in character calls for considerable maturity of outlook.

In order to see whether the influence of Outward Bound courses varied with different types of student, one particular school divided the answers among the following eight different groups of students:

(1) Students selected by the warden of the School as being the best. These included all those awarded what is called the 'Warden's Badge' at the end of the course for making the most of its opportunities.

(2) Students selected by the warden as being typical of the worst students of the year, complete failures, or those who had absconded or been sent home.

(3) Those sent by the Home Office or by the probation service.

(4) Those seconded by army, navy or air force.

(5) Those seconded by the police or the fire service.

(6) Those sponsored by industry.

(7) Those sponsored by banking or commerce.

(8) Those sponsored by parents, schools, L.E.A.s or private associations.

As expected there were some striking differences between the views of good and bad students. These may be summarized as follows:

(i) Both groups had the same proportion (15 per cent) completing a full secondary school education, i.e. previous education appears not to influence ability to profit from the course.

(ii) None of the best students had been pressed to attend but a quarter of the worst students fell into this category.

(iii) All except one of the worst students claimed that they had been badly briefed.

(iv) The worst students were much less appreciative of the mental and cultural activities of the course than the best. The same applied also to appreciation of the religious services.

(v) The greatest difference between the best and worst students occurred in relation to the degree to which a course was followed up afterwards. None of the worst students were promoted and the numbers joining youth clubs, giving community service or continuing outdoor activities was between a half and a third fewer than in the case of the best students.

(vi) The percentage of the worst students who were anxious to attend an extension course was much less (at 40 per cent) than the normal percentage of 85 per cent, but it was still surprisingly high.

(vii) All the best students thought an Outward Bound course would influence them for life as against only 70 per cent for the worst students, but again this percentage is surprisingly high.

When the views of the other six chosen groups were studied, very few consistently different points of view could be abstracted. Only two differences were sufficiently marked to be worthy of mention. It was individuals sponsored by the Home Office who expressed the greatest appreciation of the quality of teaching, the degree of individual help given by instructors, and the varied and valuable equipment possessed by the schools. This difference must express to some extent their critical view of their experience in Approved Schools or Detention Centres.

The second striking figure was that of 100 per cent for the students from industry and from school who expressed a strong wish to be invited to a second or extension course compared with 70 per cent for the other groups.

Such figures as these are striking, but they must be studied in conjunction with the attitudes of the worst students and the failures. This group is small, being not more than 2 or 3 per cent of those entering courses (and it would be surprising if the courses suited every adolescent). Some fail to identify themselves with the objects of a course and so fail to respond to its obligations and challenges. A more detailed study than was possible in a work extending only over two years might reveal to what extent failure is due to causes over which the promoters of Outward Bound have no control and to what extent to defects in the courses themselves. Every educational institution would profit from a careful case-history study of its failures, but I have never heard of such a study being made. The original standard courses at an Outward Bound School might not have been the best form of adolescent education for all teenagers but as each year now produces new types of course, and no less than ten different types are now available, the degree of failure to meet educational needs must steadily decrease.

Another facet of the work of Outward Bound Schools is their influence on other forms of adolescent education and the question of 'adventure training' in general. The first and clearest example of a corporate influence of this kind showed itself in the setting up by the army of Outward Bound Schools in Wales and Norway to meet its own training needs. All the permanent instructors at the Army School have completed at least one course as temporary instructors at an Outward Bound School, some have had experience as permanent instructors in the schools, and the director is a man with considerable Outward Bound experience.

The Army School differs in two respects from the Trust's Schools. Its courses are shorter—and all the evidence seems to suggest that the main value of an Outward Bound Course only comes at its end. And there is a lack of the rich mixture of vocational and educational types of student which is a central feature of Outward Bound courses. On the other hand, in the army, a period of Outward Bound training can be geared closely to the general training of the Junior Leader Units in which military training, trade training, physical education and general education all play a part. Moreover, the problem of a follow-up of an Outward Bound course does not arise. As a result of the integration of courses at the Army Outward Bound School with general training it is possible to ensure that its entrants arrive physically fit, with a good knowledge of map-reading and considerable outdoor experience, so that the course can be shortened without serious loss. The success of the Army Outward Bound School in Wales has led to the establishment of a second school in Norway, where the mountains, sea, and snow make adventure training even more exacting and varied than in Wales. There are, nevertheless, some regiments, such as the Parachute Regiment, that prefer to send their potential leaders to a standard course at an Outward Bound School rather than to one of the Army Schools.

The influence of the Outward Bound idea on naval training has been no less than in the army. As long ago as 1954 a Mediterranean Fleet Outward Bound Association was set up to promote Outward Bound courses organized as part of the training exercises of ships of that fleet. A handbook of training was written and a central store of equipment set up.

The natural resources of the Mediterranean make very adventurous courses possible. Within the reach of ships in harbour there is skiing in the Maritime Alps, climbing in Corsica, Sicily, and Sardinia, and rock-climbing in Malta and Gibraltar; and long-distance expeditions between ports can be made by routes that are demanding and full of potential educationally.

These are direct examples of the influence of the schools, and in the development of this work as in the development of the schools overseas the British Schools have been very generous in accepting Outward Bound staff for training and in seconding their own instructors for training and development work in new schools. There has also been a much more widespread and diffused influence. This has shown itself in the increasing number of Adventure Centres set up by Local Education Authorities for use mainly in the summer months by the youth service and by schools. The list of institutions, schemes, and organizations that owe something to the steadfast development of the Outward Bound idea by the Trust would be very long. Some obvious titles spring to the mind at once—Brathay Hall in the Lake District, and the Endeavour Scheme of the National Association of Youth Clubs are obvious examples.

One of the organizations that seconds a high proportion of its recruits to Outward Bound courses is the police, yet only a small number of the police forces of the country have (unwisely, one might think) set up a Police Outward Bound School in the style of the Army Schools.

The reason for this was expressed by a police inspector
to the author in the words:

'The idea of the majority of Chief Constables is to get
recruits and junior officers out of the dangerously
closed circle of the police world, to try to broaden their
minds and interests, to help them to become less self-
conscious and to mix freely with people from other
walks of life. They feel that as a result they have a
greater understanding and tolerance and a greater
realization of their limitations. Nor are we afraid of the
idea of training for leadership. As a young policeman,
confronted with my first accident, I found people old
enough to be my parents looking at me to see what I
would do. A young policeman has got to be a leader
of some kind.'

I asked scores of young policemen and policewomen at
Outward Bound courses if they had found any one thing
of special value to them 'as policemen' in the courses. All,
without exception, spoke of the immense value of being
able to live for a time as a civilian and to drop the 'police'
attitude towards their fellows. They all said that they had
come to realize the grave temptation of thinking of themselves as a group 'apart'.

Such a temptation is dangerous to the police of a
democratic state for the 'police state' can develop very
easily from very small beginnings. The members of a
police force are armed, potentially at least, with great
powers over the freedom of their fellow citizens. They
are given unusual powers and the Actonian dictum that
all power corrupts is as true of police power as any other.
England, Scotland, and Wales are among the very short
list of countries of the modern world where police power
is rarely abused. It is impossible to pick up a daily newspaper today without reading a story of police ruthlessness
somewhere—of detention for years without trial, of
torture, sometimes to the point of death, in the course of

police interrogation, and of police brutality either exercised on their own account or in the service of a dictator or group of dictators of a police state where human rights have been reduced to a minimum.

The violence associated with protest movements and separatist nationalisms in the modern world tends to produce, by reaction, violence from the forces of law and order. It is from such beginnings that a police state can grow. One of the important safeguards against such a growth in the democratic state is the organization of periods of purely 'civilian' training for members of its police force.

When my own survey of the influence of Outward Bound courses on these students was drawing to a close the statistics I had gathered forced me to consider how these could be explained in terms of the educational strategy and tactics employed by wardens and their staffs in the common pattern of education which I had observed taking so many different forms in different schools.

10. TECHNIQUE AND PERSONALITY

Looking back on his many years of work with Outward Bound Courses, Jim Hogan writes:
'It was not only that boys were given the chance to assess other people in situations of strain. They could not fail to re-assess themselves. There must have been few who viewed all of the activities with equanimity. Month after month as I gave the introductory talk and outlined what would be expected by the end, I was conscious of the politely restrained derision and incredulity with which it was all received. Yet, equally, month after month, the magic somehow worked and each normal sample of young men visibly grew in confidence and determination. In some cases the effect was dramatic; the intensity of experience undoubtedly caused a boy to face life with a new spirit and attitude. More often however one was well content to know that a boy had been caused to "raise his sights", to believe that given faith in himself and the courage to face a situation he was capable of more than previously he had conceived as possible.'
I met this point of view so often in my discussions with the more articulate students and the more reflective instructors that I began to look more closely at the different techniques used in the schools to achieve the aims they had set themselves. In the end I came to the conclusion that it was a particular combination of six

techniques that produced the results which, as my work proceeded, had so surprised me.

My other quotation is taken from a letter which I read in the course of my follow-up of a number of cases of failure at an Outward Bound course. I had begun to think that the surprisingly large figures I was getting for success in courses concealed some unadmitted failures. If they did, the following letter from a sponsor about one of the students made it clear that my figures for the percentage of admitted failures also included some concealed successes:

'It may be true that this boy is a failure as far as Outward Bound is concerned, but time could prove that he obtained more from his month than all the others put together.... His past background by any standards was shocking. There was only a very faint spark of hope that anything could be done with him, with his dirty, sloppy, lazy ways and his take-all-give-nothing-back way of life. A week after his return he started work and has held the job. Outward Bound gave him the gifts he most wanted—self-respect and the respect of others.'

The educational aims and philosophy of the Outward Bound School were defined quite early in its life, but this early definition has been slowly modified by practice over the years and now finds expression in the statements of aims and objectives set out in slightly different terms by each of the schools today. These differences did not surprise me because the development of creative educational ventures in Great Britain has generally proceeded far less by the attempt to institutionalize a set of logically argued aims than by an empirical advance, testing each step by results as it is taken, all being based on an intuitive understanding of the nature of human personality and of the techniques that will enhance it. Educational advance in England is always cautious in this way. Many individuals work separately and together towards a desired end, rejecting elements that lead to failure, capitalizing on success, until a new venture is consolidated, and then, usually after the event, a coherent philosophy is formulated. The elements in the educational practice of the Outward Bound Schools that have chiefly contributed towards its success seemed to me, as I reflected on my visits to them, to be six in number.

1. The Educational Use of a Country Environment

The schools are all sited in the quiet countryside, on beautiful stretches of coastline, or among mountains. Except for the Moray School, which was built as a school, all have at the centre of their working buildings what was once a large but simple family house, in a setting of parklands or gardens. Students' interviews spoke often of the value of a mere 'withdrawal' for a short period from our sprawling industrialized cities and towns. They enjoyed a period of quietness and reflection, close to nature, surrounded daily by scenes of surpassing natural beauty. The American painter Mohlzahn has presented the University of Seattle with a canvas, 'The Eclipse of Man', which is a symbolic representation of the 'Cornucopia of manufactured plenty destroying the creative spirit of man'. So often do the corrupting springs of mechanized work and mass propaganda leave the city dweller a hollow, tense, dependent creature, who cannot easily escape from the debilitating influences of political manipulation and commercialized amusement. In addition, we live in an age of violence. Eric Fromm in his book *Fear of Freedom* develops the idea that destructiveness is the outcome of the unlived life. He writes: 'Life has an inner dynamism of its own; it tends to grow and to be expressed, to be lived. If this tendency is thwarted, the energy diverted towards life undergoes a process of decomposition and changes into energies directed towards destruction'. A

C.O.B.—5

mere withdrawal for a period from the tension of city life, from radio and television, from football match and bingo hall, does not by itself renew the springs of life when they have been dulled by artificiality, but it does make available to a good many at the impressionable and spontaneous period of adolescence the setting in which renewal may take place, and clearly often does take place.

The work of the schools has at times been criticized because of this element of 'withdrawal' from the normal urban life of the modern citizen, on the ground that it is an 'escape' from the everyday problems that press on the adolescent—problems of sex, politics, drug-taking, and violence. This question will be considered in more detail later but two things should be said here. The first is that all educational work involves an element of escape. The study of poetry, for example, in the sixth form of a city school may be a form of escape. The question which educationalists have to answer is not whether something is an escape or not but whether the 'escape' element in their work leads later to the active attack on social problems or to evasion. The second thing to be said, and it will be followed up later, is that if this balance between 'escape' and 'attack' in the work of the Outward Bound has been weighted too much on the side of 'escape' (and the figures of roughly one-third of Outward Bound students who are led on to join youth organizations and to find some form of active community service do not support this) then the development of the City Challenge courses will quickly restore the balance, or may even, in their deep urban involvements, swing the balance too far the other way.

2. The Development of the Whole Person

Outward Bound Schools differ from similar educational enterprises in the breadth and depth of their aim, which is no less than the development of the whole person. The time-table of a school is a measure of its means to achieve this aim. Its order, planning, and integration provide a rigid framework that gives assurance to students. Its dynamic nature is to be seen in its arrangement of periods of growth and of consolidation. Its skills and experiences are used not as ends but as means for producing personal development, by the contriving of a series of experiences which, in their difficulty, hazard, and often unpleasantness, call for powers of the will and of decision. Occasionally students find that this life of decision is so hard compared with the softness of their normal lives in our affluent society that they give up the struggle. These are the failures; and a degree of failure is the price that must be paid for so great a measure of success. There are many helps provided for the student to succeed. Physical skill and the discipline of safety are both used to cast out fear. A glimpse of the effects of service to the old, to children, to the locality or the nation overcomes self-pity. But no degree of sympathy or understanding does or ought to prevent burdens from falling squarely upon the shoulders of students and of being either accepted or rejected. Experiences are provided, plus opportunities to reflect on the value of such experiences. When this has been done, the rest must be left to the students themselves.

3. The Use of Group Methods of Learning

Personality develops fast when an individual is a member of a group in which the needs of the individual are paramount and seen to be paramount yet personal relationships are continually stressed. Above all the life of the group must be characterized by a strong atmosphere of affection and trust if personality is to grow.

This is the life which the staff of every school tries to generate in each of its courses. That it succeeds in doing so is partly a matter of personal dedication to the ideals of the movement by the warden and his staff and partly of the use of the right techniques of group living. Some of these techniques are worthy of mention. The Outward Bound Trust takes great care in appointing its wardens and having appointed them leaves them very free of external control to be both administrators and artists in the creation of their school life. The warden of a school needs this freedom if he is to be creative but he also needs both the support and criticism of one or two objective bodies. He gets this from a School Board of Directors (and particularly its chairman) and from the Central Trust in London. The position of a warden might be a lonely one but for the regular conferences of wardens arranged by the Trust, which enable him to share his problems with his peers; and also for the light guiding hand of the Trust itself.

The instructors in a school are chosen and appointed on two main grounds—they are highly skilled and qualified teachers in their own field, and their past experience must make it clear that even before the age of thirty they already possess some of the qualities of character and understanding which makes them successful with young men and women between the ages of sixteen and twenty.

The numbers with which the warden and his staff are concerned are not a matter of chance. The optimum course is composed of about 100 members. It is just possible for a warden to know all of these by name and some very well by the end of a course. The organization of each course falls mainly on the shoulders of a small executive group of five—the warden, deputy warden, bursar, secretary, and matron; small enough and yet comprehensive enough to deal with the many practical problems of students individually. At a smaller group level than this the relationships between the instructor and his group of twelve students is close and individual.

Each student is aware of the importance given to him as an individual by the technique of arranging formal instructor-student interviews at the beginning, in the middle, and at the end of a course. At these interviews his personal development before, during, and after a course is discussed with frankness and often in considerable depth. The writing of the long individual reports at the end of the course, which sponsors find so valuable and wardens so time-consuming, underlines the importance of the individual to the school staff. To balance this individualism, the watch or patrol of about twelve members emphasizes group unselfishness and the need for the stronger or more skilled to help the weaker or less skilled. This interplay between the individual and the group is assisted by a carefully limited amount of inter-group competition and by the contrast of solo and group expeditions. Finally, the regular morning assembly integrates individual and group into the feeling of unity of a whole school.

Over and above the interplay of individual and group activity in each school, wardens develop a staff group with a very strong family feeling between its members. A staff group of about thirty is the right number, and there is a happy relaxed feeling about the schools, partly produced by the way in which dogs, children, wives, younger women, servants, daughters, and visitors wander freely in and out of the predominantly male activities of the schools. This central warmth of community life spreads out into the spartan boarding-school life of the students and in the majority of cases is in sharp contrast to all previous experiences of community life in day school, factory, office, or Borstal. This atmosphere, which students are quick to catch, is one in which they are accepted as individuals on their own merits and in which people care for each other with no regard to financial profit or status-seeking. In some cases individuals spoke of this as almost their first experience of human affection. It was particularly valuable to the small percentage of members who had been sent to courses by the Home Office and who mostly were suffering from one form of personal insecurity or another.

In this group life of the school, the principle of self-government is used both in the organization of the patrol or watch and in the school itself. After the first week, the group elects its five 'officers' of captain, vice-captain, quartermaster, steward (responsible for food), and dispenser (responsible for first-aid and safety measures) by secret ballot. Meetings of wardens, instructors and patrol captains form a steering committee for the course, which makes it an operation more democratic than hierarchic. It is this that makes it possible to dispense with rules and to deal with problems of discipline by discussion rather than the imposition of sanctions.

Surprise was frequently expressed to me at the great freedom from formal discipline found in the schools and the lack of sanctions to maintain discipline, except the realization that at the end of the course the Outward Bound Badge might not be awarded or that, in an extreme case, a student might be sent back to his school or place of employment. Over and above all this there was appreciation by students that the discipline of a skill and the natural authority of highly expert instructors gave to the course an order and discipline which, after a week, was accepted as reasonable and natural, and which, in all the schools, was firm without being repressive.

There were many appreciations by students of this democratic aspect of life in a school. The absence of class or functional distinctions between instructors, cooks, gardeners, cleaners, and others serving the needs of the school disposed quickly of some students' initial potential hostility, particularly where these students had been seconded or pressed to come and expected to find in a school some 'establishment' against which they could 'protest'.

4. The Discovery of Unrealized Physical and Mental Potential

The emphasis on the discovery of physical potential, previously unrealized, derives in the first place from the acceptance by each student of the training conditions of no smoking or drinking. This negative requirement is supported by the keeping of medical records of weight and physical condition by a doctor and of the general oversight of health by a state registered nurse or a matron with nursing qualifications.

A number of comments indicated that about one-third of the students arrived at a course lacking in self-confidence, and thinking of themselves as far from tough or with little athletic prowess or experience of outdoor activities. Their self-discovery included in all cases that of unknown physical potentiality and the ability to complete difficult and hazardous tasks. This gives a view of the work of the schools somewhat different from its 'public image' as a work only suited to the physically tough. It is nevertheless not unsuited to the physically tough, and students from the Parachute Regiment spoke to me of their being 'stretched' by the course even after a period of tough army training; but it can be and is adapted to the needs even of the physically handicapped as well.

The initial training conditions have been under discussion and modification for several years and have been applied less stringently in recent years. A minority of students, looking back on them after a year or two, would like to see them disappear. Yet almost all the students at the extension course at Moray wanted them kept or strengthened. As they said, the wonderful feeling of physical euphoria felt at the end of a course would not come to even a moderate smoker apart from this discipline. They also argued that in our age of plenty it was a valuable self-discipline to dispense completely with some comforts. My own view is that the rule about drink might be modified to allow a limited quantity of beer to be consumed in a 'canteen' period. Smoking is in a different category, because of its association with lung cancer, but even for smoking, a careful scheme of self-examined reduction down to zero by the end of the course might be a better training in self-discipline than a total ban. It would also largely avoid the danger of dishonesty; and it could be argued that lung cancer is a lesser evil than dishonesty.

In addition to these basic physical requirements there is an individualization of physical effort so that all are 'stretched', but to different degrees according to capacity. Perhaps the most important element in the realization of physical potential comes from the planned 'rhythm' given to the course by a carefully arranged time-table of 'rest periods' and 'stretch' periods that lead up, through a series of 'plateaux', to a final maximum achievement, and a final sense of physical fitness.

The development of increased self-confidence is so often mentioned by students that it must be due to many causes in addition to the confidence of well qualified instructors which is passed on to students in situations of challenge, or to the sympathetic attitude of instructors to those weak in physical skills or endowment or lacking in self-confidence.

On the negative side there is the overcoming of fear by a very strong emphasis on safety and a study of safety measures in all situations of risk; there is the defeat of fear by skill in the study of the skills of climbing, sailing, or expeditions, and by the presentation of graded challenges to developing courage as the course proceeds, for example in a graded ropes course or by a thirty-foot leap into a river inserted at a point where students are ready to face a severe challenge.

5. Participation in Community Service

Training in rescue techniques at the schools is of several kinds. Mountain rescue, coastguard rescue, surf life-saving, cliff-to-sea rescue, lake rescue, 'drownproofing', and survival swimming, all form part of it, and in addition the schools are actual rescue posts and the log-books of rescues made by boys and girls in training make very good reading. Sometimes a difficult rescue operation has in a few hours achieved more than days of school activities. This was certainly the case on the April 1966 course at Eskdale when sixty students took part in a massive rescue operation following the worst Lake District accident of all time.

The schools cannot, for lack of time, do much more than give the students a glimpse of the importance of community service but, even so, the statistics show how often a window has been opened and as a result after leaving a course a student has sought for some oppor-tunity to continue this sort of work. Certainly the inclusion of a little practical work of this kind does more than many uplifting talks. Assistance given to the work of the National Parks authorities is particularly important because it emphasizes one of the greatest problems of our time—the conservation of the natural beauty and the amenities of our land against the accelerating inroads of the 'asphalt civilization'. Wall repairs, sheep rescue, flood damage repair, are all services appreciated by the local farmers. Assistance to Local Education Authorities in the provision of adventure playgrounds, help to young over-burdened housewives and practical aid to the old and the handicapped all seem simple and limited forms of service, but their absence would omit an important element from the attempt to influence the students' personal development.

6. The Inclusion of Intellectual and Cultural Activities

The cultural and intellectual activities of the courses vary somewhat from school to school and the large degree of experimentation in this field shows that the best and final solution to this part of their work has not yet been found. In the follow-up study already described a significant number of students mentioned these activities in the space allocated to them for free comment. In many of these there was an awareness that such activities were somehow 'patched on' to the main garment of the course and so tended to be regarded as 'frills' by some students. Against this it has to be remembered that the educational level and equipment of the students at Outward Bound Schools is of so wide a range that work in an intellectual field is difficult to organize without boring the highly intelligent on the one hand and the barely literate on the other.

Several ways of dealing with this problem of range of ability have been tried. An obvious way is the free discussion group. It is important for many reasons that there should be as much open discussion of the issues of the day on a course as time allows. At the least it gives the school staff the chance to listen to the views of a younger generation and they cannot do their work without knowing what these are. In the discussions that I attended, the students spoke freely, vigorously, and with keen interest. It may be that there should be more time given to discussion and more sophistication in stimulating it. Provocation by a radio or telecast or a tape-recording could be used as well as the more general method of getting three or four knowledgeable individuals with sharp differences of view to start a discussion and to answer questions.

A second device used to overcome the range of ability problem is that found so useful in schools—the individual or group project. A particularly vigorous attack from this direction has been mounted at Ullswater and the experiment has educational value because of the approach of the warden, which is expressed in his own words:

'At Ullswater no boy is actually taught how to use his hands for project work. He is merely encouraged and inspired by his instructor to design and create something that is a product of his own brain, where his own, often latent, powers of creativity are called upon. Many a boy, considered a laggard on the physical activities, had "found" himself during the project work, often because he had eyes to see as he toiled across the mountains or down our rivers.'

The greatest value of this approach to the use of projects comes from its deliberate association with a study of the topography, ecology, history, archaeology and economy of the region round the school. There is an element of regional study in courses at all schools but it needs to be integrated at a deeper educational level with the practical exploration of the area that takes place on expedition work. I should like to see an experiment tried out at one of the schools (even if some existing elements of a course are dropped) in holding a series of almost daily sessions on regional study, followed by controlled observation on expeditions, the whole to be consolidated by discussion and analysis towards the end of a course. Aspects of topography, ecology, history, archaeology, and economy might be divided among patrols or watches so that each undertook the collection of material under a single heading and reported its work in plenary sessions. This work might be too much for the already heavily burdened instructors, but a small team of part-time teachers might be recruited locally and their work co-ordinated by an instructor. Often the English village or small town is rich in the necessary 'amateur experts'. In an initial experiment, the Institute of Education of the nearest university might be willing to lend or to second one of its extra-mural teachers, or a research worker, to break new ground in this field.

The naturalness and zest with which a regional study was incorporated into the first Luxembourg course show that it is regional studies that are the proper intellectual counterpart to physical activities. It is at once obvious that opportunities should be taken to study the language, life, work, history, and background of the citizens of a foreign country, when this is the 'region' of a course overseas, yet, to most of its students, the region in which a British Outward Bound School is set is nearly as foreign.

11. EXPANSION

Over twenty-eight years there has been a steady expansion both in the number of Outward Bound Schools in Great Britain and in the number of students who annually take part in their courses. Nevertheless, there has been a levelling off in recent years for several reasons. The very success of the schools has made many more forms of adventure training available for the young school leaver than were open to him even ten years ago. The work of the new Industrial Training Boards and the financial help available to students, and Colleges of Further Education for the provision of part-time or day-release courses requiring regular attendance, now makes it difficult for a young worker to attend an Outward Bound Course and so miss the continuity of his technical education. Local Education Authorities have had to find ways of economizing as a result of the restriction of grants from the central exchequer, as have employers with increases in corporation tax. At the same time as these forces have been operative, the costs of providing a boarding-school education for an agency that relies wholly on fees and gifts for its income has increased very steeply. So an increase in the number of standard courses is a question that needs to be looked at, not only by the Outward Bound Trust itself but by all of those who are concerned with the expansion of post-school education in Great Britain.

Primary education could be planned and widely extended by nineteenth-century prosperity, but only just; it was too often a cheap and nasty education for the sons of the labouring poor. Secondary education was inevitably more expensive. It called for more highly paid teachers, many of them university graduates, who were not very numerous. So it had to remain for a long period the privilege of a selected minority, which it still remains in countries that are industrially undeveloped or only in process of industrialization. It was not at first realized, even in some highly industrialized countries, that their new wealth was sufficient to make universal secondary education possible and that it was also essential if a steady supply of specialists and a new kind of managerial talent was to be made available.

The discovery of atomic energy and the use of electronic computers applied through servo-mechanism to the automation of industry are just beginning to produce very great wealth in a few countries and, for the first time in human history, though many have not realized it, not just secondary education but higher education for all is now a possibility. The two parts of the world where this truth has been largely accepted are the U.S.S.R. and the U.S.A. In the U.S.S.R., where higher education is geared closely, indeed some could say too closely, to economic planning, the goal has been set for universal higher education by 1980. Until 1980, the way forward chosen by the U.S.S.R. is to provide education of university quality to about half its students, by a highly organized system of correspondence, radio, and evening-class education. The Republics of the U.S.S.R. are now covered by a network of conference centres where about a million part-time students meet regularly with tutors to discuss their work.

In the U.S.A., the device used in the transition period,

before all graduates from her comprehensive high schools are able to find an institution of higher education able to accept them, has been to expand at great speed a system of regional junior colleges. In some school districts of some states all the school-leavers continue education in a junior college. Some of the public junior colleges have 2,000–3,000 students on their rolls and these always include some adults who dropped out of the educational race too early. The junior colleges provide a wide range of courses at the same general standard as are provided in the first two years of a university, partly in order that some of their graduates can go on to a full four-year university course if they wish to do so, and partly for a majority whose two years of higher studies at a junior college prepares them for the numerous specialized posts in the expanding economy of the U.S.A. A somewhat similar device to the junior college is in growing use in France where, since 1950, regional *collèges universitaires*, providing only two years of higher education, have steadily grown in number.

In Scandinavia, because of the way in which secondary and higher education have developed, a kind of higher education open to all school-leavers has been available since the first Folk High School was opened in Jutland in 1844. There are some similarities between the folk high schools of Scandinavia and Outward Bound Schools, as well as some sharp contrasts. Both provide short courses for young men and women between sixteen and twenty at boarding schools deliberately situated in the natural beauty of the countryside. In Denmark, the standard courses are of five months in winter and three months in summer. In both folk high and Outward Bound Schools there is a belief in the virtue of smallness; both engender at their country houses a pleasant, warm family atmosphere, shared in a democratic way by their 100 or so students, staff and domestic workers. The folk high schools are private schools, managed by boards of trustees, as is the case with the Outward Bound Schools, and both attract staff who are dedicated to their work to a degree not met with in other schools. In both types of school there is the underlying assumption that the basis of moral education must be found in the ethos of Christianity. Although, in a country like Denmark, a few school-leavers attend a course at a folk high school at some time in the six years after they leave school, there have been a sufficient number of schools (more than 100) for their short courses to have made a profound impression on every aspect of Danish life.

In Great Britain we have neither junior colleges nor folk high schools, but we do provide plenty of further education for our school-leavers, some much better than that found in any other country. Our system of industrial training for apprentices, for example, and the further education available to young workers in regional colleges of technology is ahead of anything provided in the U.S.A. The youth service organized by L.E.A.s through the provision of full-time youth leaders or officers who co-ordinate the work of voluntary or maintained youth clubs or organizations such as the Boy Scouts, Girl Guides, or the Red Cross is also unique in its scope and influence compared with all other countries. Quite recently, in all sections of the economy, Industrial Training Boards have been set up which will give particular attention to the training of the young worker and as these will dispose of the funds from a financial levy on their particular industry they should be able to run and equip a wide variety of training courses. These are all excellent features of our higher education, yet its pattern lacks coherence.

In the 1963 Report of the Robbins Committee we have a clear and detailed blue-print for the expansion of higher education. What we now need is another com-

mittee and another report of similar scope to deal with
the education of the 90 per cent of school-leavers who do
not go on to full-time higher education. We need plans
for the majority giving the same sort of coherence and
the same phased development as we now possess for the
minority. As part of such plans, a doubling of the present
provision of Outward Bound courses would not seem to
be extravagant or disproportionate and as my survey proceeded I increasingly came to feel that such an expansion
was desirable. Increasing the number of schools from six
to twelve over a short period would be a realistic scheme
so far as staffing is concerned, because the existing six
schools have been almost wholly responsible for training
the staff of the overseas schools as these have grown from
one to nineteen. What the Outward Bound Trust would
need to effect such an expansion would be a capital grant
for new buildings and a national quota of students' grants
to supplement the existing grants by local authorities or
the fees paid by private sponsors.

An expansion of Outward Bound Schools from six to
twelve might more than double the impact on the generation now leaving our schools, simply because forms of
education, like anything else, go unnoticed until they
reach a certain threshold figure. It is only possible to guess
what this threshold figure might be. The statistics quoted
in the Robbins Report on Higher Education and the
proposals for the expansion of all forms of full-time
courses have provided higher education for about 10 per
cent of the age group eligible for it. Of the 90 per cent
that remain, some undertake part-time courses or training
courses provided by their employers, or give their spare
time to youth or community service work, and even a
doubling of the number of Outward Bound Schools
would only mean that 1 per cent of this large proportion
of 90 per cent would, in any year, spend about a month
in an Outward Bound School. It is just possible, however,

that 1 per cent, rather than 0·5 per cent is a realistic 'threshold' figure. If any statistics of this kind or any submissions put forward in this book lead to an expansion of this order, then the work that has gone into its preparation will have been richly rewarded.

12. THE CONTEMPORARY SITUATION

It was Hamlet who said, 'Some must watch whilst some must sleep: so runs the world away'. As the pace of change quickens and the modern world 'runs away', some sleep, but others are anxious about the future for their children and watch closely the forces that are producing revolutionary change today. Most of these observers detect five trends that are likely to become stronger, and which even now influence the minds of adolescents. If it were necessary to choose five adjectives to describe these trends in contemporary society they might be the words *revolutionary, urbanized, escapist, propagandist, and secular*—or, less comforting, *violent, depersonalized, neurotic, intolerant, and materialist*. Educational initiatives need to be judged by unchanging criteria but, in addition, the question that always has to be asked is how far they will help to prepare the next generation for life in a different world from that which their teachers have known.

It is clear that we live in a revolutionary age, one similar, in some respects, to the seventeenth century. In that earlier century, men from Europe, adventurers of great courage, first settled in what they called the 'New World'. In our century, men from that New World have left the traces of their heavy boots on the grey dust of the Moon. In both centuries, fellows of the Royal Society saw no limits to research in science and technology.

In the seventeenth century, dreams of a United Christendom were fading before fierce nationalisms dedicated to armed and intolerant separatism. Then, as now, the prisons were full not only of criminals but of those whose only crime was opposition to a political opponent, or a refusal to accept the abolition of civil liberties.

Both were centuries of vivid contrasts—great wealth was flaunted while thousands starved. A burst of creativeness in science, literature, art, music and in the arts of war, went side by side with attempts to escape from the burdens of revolution and violence.

The rapid spread of the printed word in the seventeenth century changed not only education but the whole apparatus of propaganda, just as television has in our own century. In both centuries poets warned men that the world was swinging away from its firm anchorage in divine purpose. A weakened and fragmented Christian church in the seventeenth century began to be replaced by new secular religions as unlike each other as fascism and communism in the modern world.

In both centuries, new wealth and new leisure produced a permissive society which, as the meaning of life disappeared, produced not only inventiveness but boredom; not only courage but despair.

It is the revolutionary trend of our time that makes educational planning so difficult. For the young, the present is a wonderful time of excitement and expectation. They were never so free of the dominance of the middle-aged. New inventiveness, a new technology, and a new adventurousness of mind in art, music, drama, and design gives each day its own excitement. At the same time, the safety of the welfare state and the comforts of an affluent society stultify the spirit of adventure and the young experience it only at secondhand through television.

In such a revolutionary age, the two qualities of character most needed are courage and self-confidence; courage to face rapid change; courage to withstand the violence of men and their weapons of propaganda; and self-confidence to avoid the neurosis that always accompanies instability. These two qualities of character are those most often mentioned by students at Outward Bound Schools as the main gain from their attendance at their courses.

The second trend in contemporary society is the destruction of the beauty and health-giving qualities of the countryside. Few countries have so much beauty in so small a space as England, yet every year a little more is destroyed. Our country houses decay and fall, the tall trees come down, and deep woodland becomes the site for an overspill. Beyond the lanes, bulldozers ram down the old hedges; airfields flay the land bare wherever there are wide stretches and open views. There is just time to save what beauty is left, if those now leaving our schools care enough about it. One of the statistics that pleased and surprised me most was the profound influence that Outward Bound courses have in this matter; not just on a few who have been sickened by the ugliness of vast conurbations, but on all students.

Only in the year 1970, called, aptly enough, Conservation Year, was it realized that the possibility actually existed of a rich technological civilization committing suicide because its machinery and industrial wastes had begun to poison the rivers, the oceans, the air, and the natural environment of man to a degree that is irreversibly destructive. The earth has its own self-regulating purification system but it can operate only within limits. Toxic wastes can kill the bacteria that normally clean rivers and then deadly poisons flow into lakes or the sea. Lakes Geneva and Constance, once crystal clear, are turning brown and toxic with the effluent from lakeside towns and industries. The Rhine is so toxic that hardy eels can barely survive and even the great oceans of the world cannot deal with the pollution that flows into them in steadily increasing amounts. Plankton forms of life, which produce about one-fifth of the earth's oxygen, have begun to decline and this could be the start of a spiral. Millions of acres of grass and trees disappear every year below concrete and macadam and everywhere natural systems of balance and renewal are disturbed.

Fortunately there are some signs that governments are aware of these problems and are no longer content to believe that they can build bigger and bigger industrial societies with no regard for the conservation of the natural environment. In England, for the first time, a Minister of Environment has joined the Cabinet with the responsibility, as his brief described it, 'for the preservation of amenity, the protection of coast and countryside, the control of air, water and noise pollution: all of which must be pursued locally, regionally, nationally, and in some cases internationally'. The work of this minister will not be effective unless he is supported locally and regionally by a strong public opinion aware of the dangers of environmental destruction and caring passionately that the English countryside should be preserved. Only if the children from great towns and industrial areas spend some time in the country and have their attention drawn to the urgent need of conservation, only if enough of them work in National Parks and engage in environmental studies, will they begin to influence the public opinion that can make governmental action effective.

It is disastrous enough to lose one's love of simplicity, inevitable when living far from nature, but worse is the dwindling of personality that comes to those whose lives are dwarfed by the sheer size of our towns. Urbanization, industrialization, and depersonalization are inextricably linked. The size and complexity of cities today stun the mind and diminish the sense of self-respect, which inevitably leads to the loss of respect for the personalities of others. To counter this depersonalization of modern life, the Outward Bound Trust firmly maintains its devotion not to size but to smallness; to the small group and the small school.

Lack of respect for the personalities of other people leads quickly to acts of intolerance and we live in a most intolerant age. The care taken at Outward Bound Schools to arrange the widest possible mixture of individuals in each of its teaching groups—never more than one or two from a particular kind of job or school—is unique, so far as I know, in education. In many institutions, small groups may contain a good mixture of individuals, but generally this is a matter of chance; I know of none where it is so deliberately organized. This does induce a growth in understanding and tolerance, as all the figures of the students' survey demonstrate, and this may be the schools' best contribution to combating the intolerance and violence of our time.

Our hard-driving materialist society disappoints some adolescent idealists; there are others who find the pace of the 'rat-race' too relentless and seek for some escape; so for one reason or another there comes into existence a not insignificant number of 'drop-outs' from society. These young people are without ambition—indeed they rarely work, finding money from parents or the welfare state or by begging—and they wander from one sordid shelter to another. Some of them even seek to escape from the country of their birth and wander rather aimlessly to the south and east where there are, they hope, warmth and fewer police. Among the escapists there are some who, having taken flight from the harsh demands of a revolutionary age, choose the more efficient escape of drug addiction and these are finally led to the most complete escape of all—an early death. It is in wealthy countries but where many are bored that the suicide rate is the highest—and in these countries it is very high in that most privileged section of adolescents, the university students. All these forms of escape, and particularly the escape of suicide, are also positive expressions of egoism, for a blindness to see the needs of others and a refusal to help them kills compassion. The only thing that can be done for those who have lost the power of compassion and chosen the way of escape is to turn their eyes away from themselves in the direction of the needs of others less fortunately placed. This is a painful process, but one of the tasks of the educator is to keep this kind of pain alive and to revive the desire, latent in all men, to help those in distress.

The City Challenge courses which have already been described do exactly this. They force young men and women to look at the lives of those sad dwellers in the decaying centres of large cities where as J. B. Mays wrote in the journal *Education* in 1962:

'We find many different kinds of social problems in close association: a high proportion of mental illness, high crime and delinquency rates; and above average figures for infant mortality, tuberculosis, child neglect and cruelty. Here, too, the so-called problem families tend to congregate. Life in these localities appears to be confused and disorganised. In and about the squalid streets and narrow courts, along the landings and stair-cases of massive blocks of tenement flats which are slowly replacing the decayed terraces, outside garish pubs and trim betting shops, in the lights of coffee bars, cafés and chip saloons, the young people gather at night to follow with almost bored casualness the easy goals of group hedonism.'

Another characteristic of the contemporary scene is the tremendous power given to all the instruments of propaganda by the new communications technology. Mental subjugation that was impossible even ten years ago is possible today, not only because of effective means of propaganda but also because many workers spend long hours at dull repetitive work in which they find no meaning, interest, or excitement. In their leisure they naturally seek escape, either in the substitute living of television or in the reaction of violence.

The propagandist is concerned to influence the individual or the group at all costs, whereas the educator is concerned that those influenced are stimulated to seek to understand for themselves the reasons why they think or act as they do and why they might change their ideas or their actions. It is the propagandist who makes all the effort and hopes only for passivity and inertness from his victims. The educator, on the other hand, puts his pupil in touch with his environment, and then leaves him free to exert himself, to seize his opportunities and to exert initiative. To the propagandist the individual is regarded as an entity with a resistance to be broken down. Individuality of thought and action is therefore suspect in institutions or societies where control is exercised by propaganda.

Some critics of Outward Bound Schools speak of them as though they were propagandist centres mainly aimed at the production of a leader group. It is true that leaders of integrity are needed as much in a democracy as in an autocracy, and there should be no attempt to avoid the kind of character training which promotes good leadership; but in a democracy 'discriminating followers' are as much needed as wise leaders. I found in the Outward Bound Schools a good balance between the emphasis on character development for the leader and for the discriminating follower. Small group work, self-government, and open discussion are the most important educational ingredients for those who are in danger of falling victims to the modern propagandist. They are techniques that are essential in democratic education if young people are not to become the slaves of modern 'collectives' such as the political party, the race group, or even the peer-group.

In a talk to teachers in Tel Aviv in 1939, just before the slaves of the race-collective in Germany began their terrible five years of destruction of European civilization, the philosopher Martin Buber said:

'A section of the young today is beginning to feel that something important and irreplaceable is lost to them— personal responsibility for life and the world. These young people do not yet realise that their blind devotion to the collective is not a genuine act of their personal life; they do not realise that it springs, rather, from the fear of being left, in this age of confusion, to rely on themselves, on a self which no longer receives its direction from eternal values. This is where the educator can begin and should begin. He can awaken in young people the courage to shoulder life again. He can teach those who drift into a craving for aimless freedom that discipline and order are starting points on the way towards self-responsibility.'

The final characteristic of modern society that must be mentioned is its 'permissive' nature. Anything goes. The old conventions, courtesies, moralities, and reverences disappear. Short-term pleasures are pursued to the defeat of permanent happiness. Even happiness itself is taken as the ultimate pursuit. It is true that a kind of happiness can be found by some as a result of just lying in the sun; but there is a *quality* of life that always lies beyond the mere fact of life. Shakespeare, in the 'permissive' society of his own time, defined this quality of life in four lines of poetry that express his own rejection of the philosophy of hedonism:

'Love's gentle spring doth always fresh remain
Lust's winter comes ere summer half be done.
Love surfeits not; lust like a glutton dies;
Love is all truth; lust full of forged lies.'

An important rejection in the educational philosophy of the Outward Bound Schools is the rejection of hedonism. This is symbolized by the spartan simplicity of their community life. The softening influence of modern permissiveness is also reduced by a discipline that rests firmly on the belief that freedom can only be secured within a framework of order in which responsibilities are accepted because they are shared. It is only a short step from the awareness of these truths to the discovery or rediscovery of those eternal values which give direction to the self. This is accepted in the declared spiritual basis of education in the schools. It must also be the reason why so many of those who teach in them or who serve them, in one way or another, strike the visitor to a school as deeply committed to their work.

Nowadays it is rather outdated to talk about character training, and if you do you are haunted by the spectres of countless Victorian headmasters intoning their platitudes at speech days without end. Yet, very briefly, it is character training that has been the aim in the minds of all those who, over nearly thirty years, have given their time and energy without stint to develop from small beginnings the six Outward Bound Schools of Great Britain and the nineteen schools overseas.

There are times when I am inclined to dismiss character training as an outmoded educational aim, but every time there comes back to my mind some poignant phrase that I first heard on the lips of an ex-prisoner of the concentration camp of Auschwitz, as I went into Germany in the summer of 1945. He called it 'the lesson of the open fire'—and other survivors of Auschwitz have written of it since. A description of this 'lesson' may be the most appropriate way of concluding my final chapter.

'In cold winter nights at Auschwitz each prison blockhouse where men starved to death in the serried bunks had before its open door a lighted brazier. It was always tempting to rise and be near the fire. But it was fatal. A prisoner might begin by lying some distance from the fire, but in time the fire drew him like a magnet; he would go closer to the flames until finally he would get as near as possible. Then, sooner or later, the contrast between the comfort of the fire at night and the stark coldness of morning roll-call became too much for emaciated bodies and bludgeoned minds to bear. It was then only a matter of time before it killed him.

'Every prisoner knew this but many were unable to resist the temptation. If a prisoner regularly left his bunk at night to be near the fire, the others knew that he had decided, even if he had not faced the decision himself, that extinction was better than torture without hope. Against this, only one thing prevailed—character—cleverness, learning, creativeness all went down—only character prevailed.'

INDEX